A
COUNTRY BUSMAN

by

John Hibbs

DTS Publishing

First published 2003

ISBN: 1 900515 30 X

Published by: DTS, PO Box 105, Croydon, UK.

Printed by: RPM Print & Design, Chichester.

© John Hibbs 2003.

British Library Cataloguing in Publication Data. A catalogue record for this book is available from the British Library.

INTRODUCTION

I wrote this book, in a sense, to repay some old debts from the past. I hope it will entertain the reader, as a story, and a true one; it may - as I very much hope - contain some lessons not unhelpful for the business of running buses and coaches today. But my years of management were rewarding, absorbing and largely happy, so that is why I felt I should try to discharge my indebtedness to those who made them so.

This is the story of two young men who, in February 1956, took over an old-established coach business, and of the background and evolution of that business. Because I survived and my partner, Bert Davidson, didn't, the story is seen through my eyes; the story of how our venture prospered and of the circumstances, both national and personal, that brought it to an untimely but honourable close. On the way it is a month-by-month account of what it is like to manage a country bus firm.

I hope that there is something here for the general reader; for all who have an interest in the bus and coach industry; for the student of business history; and especially for all those who know and love the villages and towns of south Suffolk and north-east Essex, where the Corona coaches ran. As I have said in another book (*The Country Bus*), it is "God's own county", whichever side of the river Stour you are.

I dedicate this book to my late mother and to my wife, who loved her so much. (The reader should note that, since my earlier marriage failed, it is not my present wife who is referred to in these pages).

John Hibbs
Birmingham, 2003

ACKNOWLEDGEMENTS

Help with preparing this book is gladly acknowledged to the late Eric "Toby" Axten; to those who have contributed photographs; to staff at the Eastern Area Traffic Commissioners' Office at Cambridge; and at the (then) National Union of Agricultural and Allied Workers; to Alan Phillips of Sudbury and Alf Wakeling of Brightlingsea. Special thanks are due to the late George Carruthers for his interest and for contributing the Preface. I have been permitted the use of copyright material by the Omnibus Society and the PSV Circle, to whom thanks are also due. The author and publisher have taken all necessary steps to identify and acknowledge the prints used and would apologise to anyone whose claim has been inadvertently overlooked.

A COUNTRY BUSMAN

Contents

PREFACE

By the late George Carruthers

The experience of a private bus operator in the 1950s and 1960s may seem somewhat remote to an industry which has subsequently seen extensive changes in ownership, organisation and statutory control. Yet with political involvement at national and local level now highlighted by the outcome of deregulation and privatisation there are common factors, and country areas still need country busmen. Thus today's operators and students should find much of interest in this book, which is more than biographical.

My interest, and my agreement to contribute a preface, is more personal, since I have known the author for some time, since the days when my Area responsibilities for the Eastern Counties Omnibus Company overlapped Corona. My perspective was that of the regional operator to an area of thriving market towns with attractive deep rural communities, depending much upon local operators for transport to workplaces, markets, shops and schools. Eastern Counties' interest was more on main interurban routes to centres such as Bury St Edmunds and Ipswich from market towns such as Stowmarket or Sudbury. All operators were jealous of their routes, many being long-established family concerns, and resort to the Traffic Courts was frequent if any encroachment threatened, with a particular watch on the growing tendency to extend Excursion & Tour licences for special events, likely to draw off service passengers.

When John Hibbs and the late Bert Davidson took on Corona the post-war boom was waning, with cuts particularly on rural routes, with the same situation leading to railway branch line closures. I well remember spending much time at local Council meetings, explaining the reasons for changes in both services and fares, endeavouring to avoid objections. This in spite of the fact that regional operators had some scope for improvements in urban services (as in Bury St Edmunds), and often could achieve economies by utilisation of new, higher capacity vehicles at lower frequencies. Certainly network operators were pleading in the Traffic Courts the need to protect good routes to enable cross-subsidisation of rural routes in particular. At times this undoubtedly weighed against efforts of operators such as Corona, trying to expand or vary services, and led to their view that the licensing system was biassed and restrictive. But regional operators, mainly state-owned, were considered by many to have some obligation to maintain networks, and there were no financial aids, not even for railway replacements. The recognition of the cost of social benefits from maintaining unremunerative services did not come until the 1968 Transport Act and subsequent Local Government Acts.

As Corona found, there really was little return from expansion, and perhaps like others they delayed tackling the underlying question of costs. For many, good bus and crew schedules and staff allocation were the basis of economic operation, leaving costings to company averages. I well remember being given each four weeks revenue statistics for each service, but only company average costs over a few main headings. But at local depot level we did begin to extract at least direct operating costs to seek the best economies. Progress overall in full costing was not helped by the acceptance and grant of fares applications as 'blankets' over all services, on a mileage basis against company costs.

It may seem odd to readers that when Corona was for sale little interest was shown by local or regional operators in acquisition, if only to eliminate a competitor. We at Eastern Counties did have a detailed local examination, but there was no enthusiasm for more rural operations. However, purchase of the London express routes was recommended, perhaps jointly with Eastern National, and I regretted that this was not pursued, as I suspected that Mulley of Ixworth, in spite of statements to the contrary, was awaiting a break-up sale, seeing here a way to improve and extend his Bury St Edmunds based services. Much time had been spent in Traffic Courts resisting Mulley applications, although these were often supported by a coach-load of supporters, if not always good witnesses. These suspicions were justified, and as the author records Eastern Counties took over from Mulley later at an enhanced price.

The unfortunate end of Corona arose perhaps most from an over-stretched financial situation, difficult to sustain against a falling market. It was certainly not, as this book illustrates, from any lack of enthusiasm or dedication from all staff, and many, if not enough, loyal passengers, who had been well looked after. This account will help many to understand the background to the author's advocacy for private ownership and a deregulated commercial market, such as has now developed following the 1985 Transport Act. I am sure the Corona experience has helped John in his subsequent career and leading role, in the study and teaching of transport matters, and road transport in particular. This is just as essential for operators and their customers on whose welfare the industry exists.

George Carruthers OBE FCIT
West Harnham, Salisbury, 1989

Chapter One

PROLOGUE:
WHY IT HAD TO BE BUSES

They say a traffic man has to be born that way. Family tradition has it that my own first word was 'bus': as to that, I cannot say, but I know that trains and buses fascinated me from a very early age. Just when and why buses started to outweigh trains I cannot remember either, but I can relive still the satisfaction of running services round the garden paths with a mixed fleet of push-chairs and wheelbarrows at about the age of eleven.

Later I would do the same with Dinky Toys on an old table, and then came the development of imaginary operations using sheets of the one-inch Ordnance Map - whole timetables with carefully constructed car-workings all set out with a Blick typewriter that I bought at the age of 18. By that time the thing was an obsession and one that lasted until the reality of operating an actual business brought me down to earth.

We lived in Brightlingsea, with its branch line that followed the river and sometimes we went to Colchester by train; sometimes on Berry's bus. When I started at the Grammar School I got to know all of Berry's buses and the staff. Pride of the fleet was the *Dorothy*, a rare example of a named vehicle, which I learnt later on had been bought to run a service to London that was never authorised. It will always be associated for me with Bill Farington, the conductor who kept us boys in order with a clip to the side of the head with his ticket rack. He needed to, at that. The 4.20pm from Colchester rarely carried a conductor and keeping order was a problem - on one occasion I can remember having to walk the three miles home from Thorrington Cross, when we were all turned out. That journey did not last long after Eastern National took over and we all had to leave school early to get the 4.05pm on the regular headway instead - large firms cannot afford to cater for individual needs, whereas the Berry family lived in Brightlingsea and West Mersea.

I sometimes wonder whether the roots of my transport interest may go further back. E. P. Dickin's history of Brightlingsea records that an ancestor of mine, who kept the *Swan* in High Street, ran a carrier's cart to Colchester in the nineteenth century and there was a motor bus operator at St. Osyth of the name of Blyth, which was my mother's family name. Even more significant, perhaps, is my grandfather's interest in Thames Barges – the fleet of Jarvis and Hibbs, of Colchester, included such vessels as *Anglia, May* and *Tintara,* and in the summer, after *Anglia* had refitted, there was the annual 'barge picnic'. The day would be spent cruising in the Colne and Blackwater estuaries, with food and drink for all (and quoits in the hold, as a game for the boys). Then each of us in turn would be given a trick at the wheel, under the supervision of Captain Ventress – I must have been 12 when I first learned to handle a barge under sail.

Holidays meant going to London. Splendid trams ran through Willesden Green, with interlaced track in Walm Lane and there was the London bus map on which to trace out routes. Or we went to Birmingham, with different trams, for which I still feel a great nostalgia. Wherever we went, I was intensely aware of the transport, so that I have a multitude of memories of the buses, trains and trams of the 1930's. Colchester, of course, was a town rich with different bus and coach liveries, as well as its own brand of transport – the open-top trams that I can just recall and then the rather peculiar buses that replaced them.

The bus park in St John's Street was a place of great fascination. Buses of every colour were lined up, with a variety of makes that we have long since lost. Destination indicators have always had a certain magic for me and one of the oddest was the prism-shaped board carried by the *Primrose* buses, which slung in two triangular brackets from the front canopy, so that one face could be turned to the front – the faces read MERSEA, COLCHESTER and PRIVATE. Then there were the Eastern Counties buses on the Ipswich service, with a stand at the end of the back row: the double-deckers (still none too common)

BELOW: The author's salt water background appears in this picture of the family business at Brightlingsea. The text formed a panel on the reverse. *(Author's collection)*

YACHTING.

Dear Sir,
We have the following Sails and Gear for sale cheap, equal to new. Jack-yard topsails, Jib Topsails, Jibs, Spinnackers, Trysails, etc., including new suit by Lapthorn for 110 ton Yawl, never bent. Also Capstans, Chain, Logs, Binnacle Compasses, Rigging Screws. Two Jarman's Patent Steering Gear, etc., from Yachts of 15 to 200 tons. Liquid Fuel Launch, cost £450, for sale, £175 or offer. We shall also be pleased to quote you for any new **Sails** or Stores you may require.

Specialities : Yachtsman's Rubber Boots, **16/9 per pair.**
Special Smart Boot, Pebbled Legs, with Special Lining.
Windproof Riding and Side Lamps.
Varnishes, 8/- 12/6 16/- 18/- gallon.

PANNELL & HIBBS, Brightlingsea.
Est. 1882.

would come on a tight lock, which made them tilt frighteningly and a minute or two later there would be a resounding *clang* as the bible destination board was changed. None of this was lost on my schoolboy enthusiasm.

So it was not surprising that I found my way into the bus business. In 1945 I met Eric Axten, who was to become a lifelong friend and fellow enthusiast and whose draughtsmanship has improved several of my books. From him I learnt about other bus companies, including one that he had just heard of, south of Cambridge. So I wrote away and received a very businesslike timetable from a company called Premier Travel. At that time too I started seriously collecting timetables and those were vintage years for such a hobby. It was an exploration, finding new companies and watching each day's post to see what new acquisitions would arrive. Sometimes it was a frustration, too – Midland Red sent nothing but sheaves of leaflets and the Whippet company at Huntingdon sent posters that referred to a timetable booklet that must have been pre-war and that I have never had the pleasure of seeing.

It was an exploration of history, too, helped by joining the Omnibus Society, which periodically auctioned off surplus material from its timetable collection. From the same source I borrowed TBR guides and began to understand the formative years of the bus industry. This too became an obsession, which I eventually brought to an end in 1972 by presenting my collection of timetables to the Omnibus Society, along with extensive runs of 'Notices and Proceedings' for the Eastern and Metropolitan Traffic Areas.

At the same time I was developing traffic skills that were to prove useful later on. I worked out the timetables and car workings for an imaginary operator based at Brightlingsea, spotting various routes that had been left unserved. It pleased me years later to see Donald MacGregor put some of the services on! Unlike some enthusiasts, I was never 'vehicle mad' – from the first it was the traffic side that fascinated me and even today I cannot pick up a timetable without wanting to sit down and analyse the car workings, or ask why some obvious facility has not been offered to the public.

After six months working in Oxford, which introduced me to the high vehicle standards associated with the National Electric Construction Company, I went to London, and while working at University College Hospital I discovered in the neighbouring mews one of the oddest transport terminals, where the smart blue double-deckers of Hicks Bros. of Braintree came and went on what was to all intents and purposes an express coach service. Not far away was the newly reopened Kings Cross Coach Station, where I saw my first Corona coach, along with those of Jennings and Burgoin's Grey Pullman, as well as Sutton and Grey-Green on the Clacton routes. I still think that one of the most cynical interventions of the government in transport was the closure of that ideally placed station – I believe it was acquired under some emergency power to serve as a depot for a film company which needed it for the export trade; that it was never used by them, but was subsequently taken over by the Post Office, which occupies it today. Whenever I pass it I breathe a curse on all concerned, as I recall how much we would have benefited the public if Corona could still have used it in my own operating days!

In 1947, I returned to Birmingham to work for a degree in social studies at the University, still mad about buses. I was engaged by then and a fellow student produced a telling Clerihew—

> *We know a cuss*
> *Who's in love with a bus*
> *I wonder if his lassie*
> *Has a very nice chassis*

– I had to admire the skill of composition, even while being embarrassed by the sentiments! Fortunately I was not the only one to be lampooned and I was regarded as a useful source of travel information. The course was divided between the Edgbaston Campus and the Edmund Street buildings in the city and the journeys between were by tram – we soon discovered the art of descending the front staircase at Navigation Street and landing on the bell trip, to the driver's distaste. (If you missed and landed on the sanding trip the effect was disappointing).

My career owes more than I can say to three men whom I met through the Omnibus Society at the time: Bert Davidson, Arthur Lainson and Gilbert Ponsonby. In the spring of 1948, having been told that the Managing Director of Premier Travel was a fellow member of the OS, I walked into the office in Cambridge and introduced myself, asking if I might see Mr. Lainson. It was in fact he who was sitting at the counter and he said, 'Just wait while I finish this and we'll go for a coffee'. We went to the Milk Bar round the corner in Market Hill and I started to learn seriously about the industry. There have been few managers who have had greater sympathy for the bus enthusiast than Arthur Lainson, surely one of the leading enthusiasts himself.

My degree course required me to spend the two summer vacations doing at least six weeks 'practical work' and I suggested I should go to work for Premier. This was approved, provided I also did something more directly related to Social Studies, so I spent part of the time at the Village College at Linton. In my second year I had to prepare a dissertation and I based this on my experiences that summer and called it 'The place of the motor bus in the local community'. No-one in the department knew much about the subject, so I worked on my own, using material and techniques from the Institute of Sociology at Ledbury, which had been responsible for a placement scheme – a social survey of Braintree – that I undertook in the spring of 1949. Gilbert Walker, who was one of the few transport academics of that day, gave me a viva voce examination, during which we talked of other matters, but the work must have been acceptable.

In the second summer vacation I went back to Premier for a time, although my placement was with Edgar Anstey in London, working on a scheme for identifying 'value contours' in terms of property values. In my final year at Birmingham I decided that social work did not attract me as a career and so I asked if Premier would give me a job, which they did, as Mr. Liaison's personal assistant. I started there in August 1950 doing much the same work that I had been given during the two summer vacations and commuting from Hadstock, a village just outside Saffron Walden, which was to be my home for the next seven years. The house had been the 'Queen's Head' and

ABOVE RIGHT: Some of my friends from Premier travel days *(Author's collection)*

RIGHT: An Omnibus Society visit to Premier Travel – members going ahead to photograph a bus under what should have been too low a bridge, at Haverhill. *(Frank Wright)*

was the timing point for Weeden's Buses, which Premier Travel had taken over. After ceasing to be a pub it had been called 'Crossways', but I gave it the name of my family's farm at Thorrington, 'Goldacre'. I didn't expect to leave it again, but Corona was to change all that.

Life at Rose Crescent, Premier's little office above '*Watches of Switzerland*', with a balcony overlooking Market Hill, was never dull and I was fortunate in having found the ideal position in which to start one's career - near to the centre of things. I was plunged into Traffic Court procedure and I acquired the responsibility for publicity, where I was in my element in compiling timetables and designing maps and posters. Going round the colleges trying to get private hire work was less rewarding, both for the company and for me; salesmanship is not my strong point. I did, however, take a big part in preparing the case for the Cambridge to Oxford coach service, which later became a marked success.

If there was one thing which stimulated my later criticism of the licensing system it was our application for a Saturday summer service from Nottingham to Clacton. We presented a strong case and at lunch-time Maurice Holmes QC (later Sir Maurice), who was opposing us, offered odds that we would win. Yet at the end of the day the Chairman of Traffic Commissioners, after complimenting us on the case, refused a grant and a few months later, despite our objection, he gave the licence to Trent and Eastern National. They were supposed to need the profits to cross-subsidise their bus services, a policy that I still think is unjust and unfair on the public. Many insights into the working of the system came from the Traffic Courts at Cambridge, where Sir Alfred Faulkner was chairman. He was very good to me, helping me to find my feet as an expert witness and later as an advocate and protecting me from the fiercer attacks of the professional gentry. From him too, I learnt how the system masked the realities of commercial competition, for he had little patience with legalistic niceties and went straight to the heart of who stood to gain or to lose. I believe he was unique in never having an appeal succeed against one of his decisions.

I stayed with Premier for two years and 'learnt the trade', often in after-work discussion with Arthur Lainson in the 'Still and Sugarloaf' bar and also with Erskine MacPherson, who had joined Premier before me, from Eastern National, and was introducing new systems to the Saffron Walden and Haverhill areas. Then in 1952, as the financial effects of the increased fuel tax and the inflation that arose out of the Korean War hit the industry, the company found it necessary to cut down on staff and three of us were asked to find alternative employment. Erskine eventually went to Canada, while I took up an offer that had already been in my mind and went to see Gilbert Ponsonby at the London School of Economics about doing some research.

I had met Gilbert back in 1949, when I presented a paper at a meeting of the Omnibus Society. It was typical of him that he too should belong to the OS and go out of his way to hear an unknown young member give a talk on a subject which interested him. It was in fact my B. Com. Dissertation, which Charles Klapper had asked me to read to a meeting of the Society at the Institute of Transport. Gilbert came up to me afterwards and said how important he thought the application of Sociology to transport was going to be and to get in touch with him if I ever wanted to do some research.

I saw him again in the summer of 1952 and he advised me to apply for the Rees Jeffreys studentship. My original plan was to look at the design of bus stations, but later on I was told firmly that my experience of licensing made me better suited to work on the economic consequences of the 1930 Road Traffic Act. So in October I became a student again, attending lectures at the School on Economics and the History of Transport and going to see Gilbert for regular supervisions, while still living at Hadstock. That was a period of 'agonising re-appraisal', as the Americans used to say, when I was made to analyse the implications of licensing and to distinguish between what we now call quality and quantity control, and the system that I had learned to take for granted came to look quite different when subjected to rigorous review. With Gilbert you could never get away with loose and unquantifiable standards like 'the public interest'. He used to say, "How do you measure the public interest?" His postgraduate seminars played a big part in my education.

In 1953 my studentship was renewed for a further year and I was allowed to register retrospectively for the M.Sc. degree in Economics. This meant a lot, since I did not have an Honours degree to start with. I worked on my thesis and when it was still incomplete by the summer of 1954, Gilbert introduced me to John Whitbread, who was writing a book on the history of the Railway Police and who employed me part-time to do research for him. With my thesis completed I had a viva voce examination by the late D.N. Chester, the only previous critic of licensing and I was awarded my Master's degree at a congregation in January 1955.

Now I was faced with what to do next. I had always intended to go back into operating, but for some reason that I did not give much thought to, I never considered joining one of the combine companies. I suppose it was the Premier Travel slogan, 'Support Independent Enterprise' that summed up my attitude – that and the disdain with which we had sometimes been treated by quite senior combine men. The fact that our buses were blue instead of red or green seemed to label us as outsiders and I grew to resent their assumption that they had a sort of divine right to any traffic that was going. It came as a surprise, later on, to learn that big company managers found the same satisfaction that I did in just running buses.

I knew well enough that my own satisfaction would lie there, too. As I learnt more about the industry I became more attracted by the thought of running my own show, and before I finished at the School I had already started at the negotiations for acquiring Corona. That story belongs to Chapter Three, but the deal was drawn out (it was to be 1956 before we took over) and I had to live in the meantime. John Whitbread's research continued to occupy me, taking me to the British Railways Archives at York as well as those in London, where I first met Edwin Course. Eric Pollock, who was a fellow student at the school, had joined the Economist Intelligence Unit and I did some consultancy work for them. Then, in June 1955, I got a conductor's badge and worked for Premier again, this time 'on the back'.

The reason at the time was the pressure on their staff due to the railway strike of that summer and I had intended to get a driver's badge but failed the PSV driving test. I enjoyed conducting, though and later that summer I arranged with Frank Grice, the depot manager at Chrishall, to work three or four days a week, which with consultancy work and journalism made enough to live on. I soon became expert with the insert Setright ticket machine and came to be accepted by the full-timers on really friendly terms. There is no better way to learn a trade than to do it yourself and what I learned in six months of early starts and late finishes taught me much that would come into its own later – and that I remember with some nostalgia today.

Chapter Two

CORONA COACHES

The roots of the business

Corona Coaches, like so many rural transport firms, could trace its beginnings to the nineteenth century. The 1850 Nathan Chinery, of the village of Acton, started to operate a carrier's cart. Little is known about this business, although it seems his carrier's operations served the Belchamps – Otten, St. Paul and Walter, three villages on the Essex side of the Stour, and that a carrier called Bowers linked Acton with Sudbury. (Later on, Corona was to serve Belchamp Walter again). In due course, however, Nathan's son, Alan, came home from the army in 1919, at the age of 24 and set about to motorise his business – in all further references it should be remembered that his name was pronounced with a long 'a' in the first syllable, to rhyme with 'pay'. Like many others, Alan decided to go in for both freight and passenger traffic, as the village carriers had always done and he began with a Ford Model 'T' lorry with an interchangeable pair of bodies, one for each mode. Two years later he obtained a Chevrolet bus and since this was a period in which fleet-names were an added touch to catch the public eye, Mr. and Mrs. Chinery called their first bus *Joybelle*.

Acton could hardly be less like its West London namesake, either then or now. In 1921 it had a population of 447, its cottages strung out along the lane from Great Waldingfield to cease abruptly at the 'Crown' inn, just opposite the Chinery home. The only local employment was on the farms or in the big houses, but there was some industry in Sudbury, five miles away and the Stafford Allen (later Bush Boake Allen) works lay in the Stour valley beyond Melford, making essences for the perfume and cosmetic industry. The new business was to be a welcome

source of employment for local men in years that followed, as well as linking the village and its neighbours with the outer world.

Transport in West Suffolk and North East Essex suffered from the layout of the main line railways. Even Bury St. Edmunds, the biggest town in the area, does not lie on a direct line to London and has never had an adequate train service when compared with Ipswich or Colchester on the one hand and Ely or Cambridge on the other. The railways in the area were either dead-end spurs, or meandered across the countryside at right angles to the main flow of traffic. The first line to reach this part of Suffolk was the branch from Marks Tey which was opened to Sudbury in 1849 and the cost of building it was so great that the junction facing London was never put in, so that

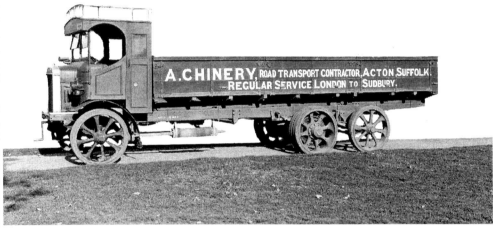

UPPER and LOWER: The London–Sudbury route was pioneered for freight in the 1920s – the Leyland could take on the railways even then. *(Author's collection)*

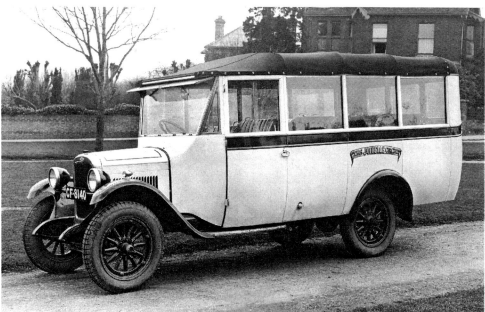

Today one of the biggest remaining operators is the firm of Theobald of Long Melford, who started in 1926. Along with Chambers, they dominate the three mile route between Sudbury and Melford, which over the years has seen a great variety of operators – **Table One (below)** lists those running in 1930.

Not all these services ran every day of course, but between them they provided a very high frequency on Thursdays (Sudbury Market) and Saturdays. The Corona contribution was small, being just the two daily journeys to and from London, which, to the chagrin of other operators, were allowed also to carry local traffic. But this is to move ahead too quickly. The village

the town was denied the potential of a full service up the main line. In 1865 a new station was opened at Sudbury and the line was extended to Long Melford and from there through Lavenham to Bury St. Edmunds and along the Stour valley to meet the existing line from Haverhill to Cambridge. Despite various abortive schemes, this was to be the end of railway building in the neighbourhood that Corona was to serve.

The starting dates for bus services in the area would need to be found by reference to local newspapers, for there was no licensing requirement in the early days. Probably the oldest firm in the district is that of H. C. Chambers and Son of Bures, who began running motor buses in 1916 and who in about 1930 acquired the service of a certain Charles Cattlin (trading under the name of Wormell) of Colchester, running from there through Bures, Sudbury, Long Melford and Lavenham to Bury St. Edmunds. This remains their principal service and to this day they are true to the convictions of the founder of the company, who would not run on a Sunday (for years this bought N. S. Rule of Boxford on to the northern end of the route, beyond Sudbury, to fill the gap). A little further away, though, a farmer called Skinner had started in 1914 to run between Boxford and Ipswich, while an operator called Beales had set up at Glemsford in 1919. These villages were later to become significant for the Corona story.

TABLE ONE:
Operators between Sudbury and Long Melford, 1930

J. Amos, Belchamp St. Paul (to Rodbridge Corner)

A. Brown, Great Cornard (licences lapsed 1931)

S. Brown, Glemsford (acquired Beales' business in 1928, sold to Long, 1943)

T. G. Brown (earlier B. T. Brown), Cavendish (sold to Wilson, 1933)

H. C. Chambers & Son, Bures

A. A. Chinery, t/a Corona Coaches, Acton (see the rest of the story)

J. W. Cook, Hartest, (sold to Theobold, 1933)

Eastern Counties Road Car Co. Ltd, Ipswich

Eastern National Omnibus Co Ltd, Chelmsford

H. G. Ham, Foxearth (to Rodbridge Corner) (licence lapsed during war years)

F. J. Honeywood, Stanstead (sold to Goldsmith, 1956)

B. K. Jennings, Ashen (to Rodbridge Corner)

A. J. Long, Glemsford (after 1938 E F Long t/a A. J. Long) (sold to Corona, 1959)

A. E. Nicholls, Clare

H. Rippingale, Gestingthorpe (to Rodbridge corner) (sold to Corona, 1950's)

N. S. Rule, Boxford

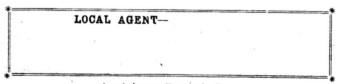
of Acton lies, not on either main road between Sudbury and Lavenham, but on the lane that connects the Waldingfield Road with Long Melford. Chambers' bus passed the Acton turning at the foot of Blackadders Hill (a name which drivers told me was genuine, for the snakes there were well known), so until the Joybelle started to run to Sudbury, Acton was without motorised connection. (I have records from those years of several operators who may have come through the village – Thomas Mayes, Blue Coaches (Lavenham) Ltd, Sudbury Motors and a man called Goddard of Lavenham, who seems to have sold his business to Blue Coaches. R. J. Bell of Long Melford certainly served Acton on Thursdays and Saturday evenings, usually going on via Great Waldingfield, but sometimes using the direct lane through Newmans Green. He gave up in 1939.)

These early years, then, saw the rapid growth of local services, carrying passengers to and from the market towns – Bury St. Edmunds, Colchester, Sudbury and Ipswich. Although they took some traffic from the railways – at Bury and Colchester the buses ran to the town centre, while the stations were some way out – they did little to improve connections to London, which were still slow and inconvenient. Country people, too, were hesitant to trust themselves to the impersonal railway and to brave the noise and confusion of Liverpool Street Station. It was here that Alan Chinery saw his opportunity and Joybelle became Corona Coaches.

Long distance road services were not new. Apart from the horse-drawn stage coaches, which gave way to the railway, the motor bus was early seen to have possibilities for more than local use and the Vanguard company of London started running to Brighton in 1905. The idea met with a setback when a Vanguard bus was involved in a fatal accident a year later, but with the end of the war new developments took place. The

LEFT: A Bedford WLT 20-seater for the London service carrying the Company name in the style that was to survive for many years.

BELOW LEFT: The luxurious interior of the Bedford shown above, illustrating Duple standards of comfort.
(Both photos author's collection)

Primrose company of West Mersea (which was mentioned in Chapter One) ran to London for a short time during a railway strike in 1919 and coastal excursions from London were firmly established in the summer of that year. However, it was on 11 February 1925 that the first true express coach service was started by the Greyhound company between Bristol and London, with individual stage to stage fares and a year-round timetable. Five years later there were 128 firms running such services in England and Wales, many of them highly competitive with each other.

Alan Chinery decided to join in. It was simple enough, provided you had the confidence: he printed a timetable, set the fares, arranged a terminal in London and appointed booking agents. Then on 6 May 1929 the Corona Coaches, Proprietor, A. Chinery, Established 1850, commenced the service between Stowmarket and London. Including a refreshment stop at 'Widford White Horse', outside Chelmsford, the coach took 4 hours 15 minutes on the up journey and 5 minutes less on the return. Thirty years later it was to take 4 hours 20 minutes, but to a terminal far short of the Charing Cross Embankment, to which the service originally ran. The 'special winter fares' introduced on 12 October 1929 were to be little changed until the post-war years: **Table Two** shows them with today's equivilant:

TABLE TWO:

Fares to London, Winter 1929-30

From	Single	Day Return	Period Return
Stowmarket, Finborough, Hitcham, Bildeston, Monks Eleigh & Brent Eleigh	5/6 (27½p)	7/- (35p)	9/- (45p)
Lavenham, Gt &Lt Waldingfield, Acton, Long Melford & Sudbury	4/6 (22½p)	6/- (30p)	8/6 (42½p)
Halstead	4/- (20p)	5/6 (27½p)	7/6 (37½p)
Braintree	3/6 (17½p)	5/- (25p)	7/- (35p)
Chelmsford	2/6 (12½p)	3/6 (17½p)	4/6 (22½p)

Certainly a day out in London for 30 pence sounds attractive today, but these fares must be seen in the context of the depressed state of agriculture and the desperately low wages of

Road Traffic Act 1930
Public Service Vehicle (Licences & Certificates) Provisional Regulations
1931
Part VII Regulation 45

To the Traffic Commissioners
(Eastern Area)
Sidney House
Cambridge

Pursuant to Regulation 45 of the Public Service Vehicles (Licences
and Certificates) Provisional Regulations 1931, the Town Council of
the Borough of Sudbury make the following representation:-

That the application of Mr Alan Arthur Chinery, of Acton,
Sudbury, Suffolk, for road service licence to run stage carriage services
all the year round on the following route:-
Your Reference F/R 16/10, be granted.

The representation is based on the following grounds:
1 .   The Area between Stowmarket and Sudbury is not served by
      direct Railway facilities.
2 .   The route suggested by Mr Chinery between London and
      Sudbury is more direct than that provided by the Railway
      service and the fares are lower.

Signed on behalf of the Town Council of the Borough of Sudbury.

T. Miles Braithwaite, Town Clerk

Town Hall, Sudbury, Suffolk

16th May 1931.

the countryside. For many years the Corona bus between Acton
and Sudbury ran on Saturday evenings two or three times each
way, to allow farm workers (who had no half day holiday) to reach
the market at the time when the stalls were selling produce at cut
prices. The minimum wages of a farm worker at the end of 1929
were set by the Suffolk Agricultural Wages Commitee at 30 shillings
(£1.50) for a 48–50 hour week, with overtime at 9d (3p) an hour
and £5.00 extra for the corn harvest. Female workers got 5d (2p)

an hour, when there was work for them, so the Corona fares were
not the bargain we might think them today.

The name Corona was chosen because Mr. and Mrs. Chinery
saw the establishment of the London service as their crowning
achievement and, by 1931, Joybelle had fallen out of use. But
the early days were not all that easy or secure. Money had been
borrowed from a relative and in that first winter traffic was hard to
come by. After a while there was pressure for the repayment of the
loan and Mr. Chinery finally had to promise that, if the service was
not profitable after a year, he would give it up. In the last few
months the traffic began to grow and the summer of 1931 saw
the service well established, as **Table Three** shows. The fare
had been raised only slightly.

TABLE THREE: Traffic Statistics for 1931 STOWMARKET – SUDBURY – LONDON										
Month	Passengers:				Veh.	Seats	Veh.	Gross revenue		
	S	DR	PR	Total	Jnys.	Avail.	Miles	£.	s.	d.
January	245	205	86	536	62	868	4,960	101.	18.	0.
February	389	158	113	660	56	784	4,480	91.	8.	0.
March	264	183	384	831	62	1,192	4,960	152.	19.	4.
April	911	488	375	1,774	76	2,116	5,920	212.	10.	8
May	1,318	610	822	2,750	116	3,280	9,120	289.	7.	5
June	1,939	866	702	3,507	120	3,840	9,600	310.	2.	1
July	1,607	1,022	1,420	4,049	132	4,224	10,400	546.	9.	6
August	1,638	1,098	2,031	4,767	164	4,888	12,320	746.	13.	11
September	1,442	1,656	1,272	4,370	140	4,608	10,800	587.	7.	10
October	2,692	902	705	4,299	144	4,488	10,440	327.	4.	10
November	1,654	693	342	2,689	120	2,640	10,800	192.	9.	3
December	1,726	546	1,018	3,290	128	2,892	11,380	349.	3.	8
Totals	15,825	8,427	9,270	33,522	1,320	35,820	105,180	£3,907.	14.	6

Why did Alan Chinery settle upon Stowmarket as the origi-
nating point for his new service to London? I have heard that
he first thought of running from Bildeston, but that Mr. O. J.
Barnard, a well known businessman of Stowmarket, suggested
the extension (and may have provided some finance - Barnards
remained a major supplier and were booking agents for the
service, until the end). With its population of some 7,000,
Stowmarket was little bigger than Sudbury and it might have

BELOW: GV1061, new in 1932, stands outside the Crown, Acton's public house and unofficial rest-room for Corona staff. The style has been established, and the London service is well displayed. *(Author's collection)*

been thought that the far greater potential of Bury St. Edmunds, an equal distance away to the north, would have made a better terminal. There seem to have been two good reasons to avoid Bury and one reason for choosing Stowmarket.

To begin with, Bury St. Edmunds to London was a route already covered by the Great Yarmouth firm of Pullman Lounge Coaches, well enough established to have their own office at 17 Craven Street, off the Strand. Then too, Cattlin had established himself as the local bus operator between Sudbury and Bury St. Edmunds and Mr. Chinery had his eye on a sound traffic potential – a London coach service that would also be a local bus at the country end. At that time there was no bus service through the villages between Lavenham and Stowmarket and that must have settled it. The fare table from the first included point-to-point stages all the way along the route (even between London and Romford, where passengers were charged 1/- (5p) single and 2/- (10p) return). In consequence, London passengers joining the coach at Sudbury could take seats vacated by those alighting there and in due course local traffic could be built up into Stowmarket to fill the seats as passengers from London left the coach in the villages.

Neither was Corona alone in this. Several other operators at this time put on London services from the area so badly served by direct railways. G. F. Burgoyne, as *Grey Pullman Saloons*, ran from Haverhill via Saffron Walden; Barnabus Jennings, an Irishman who had settled at Ashen, ran from Cavendish and Clare through Thaxted and Bishops Stortford; A. A. Akers, of Halstead, trading as *Bird Motor Services*, started from Castle Hedingham and quickly established himself as the leading Halstead – London operator; and S.Blackwell & Son of Earls Colne ran Chappel – Halstead – London, with feeder service from Coggeshall that started out going north in order to go south. Two London operators got into the act: one whose title is not recorded, used the fleet-name *Intrepid* and based two Leyland Lioness coaches at Castle Hedingham for a short time in 1929-30, running over the

THESE FOUR PICTURES serve to illustrate *"A little local difficulty"* in Hadleigh. This Leyland KPX2 with Duple 25-seat body was new in 1938 and was not sold until 1953. *(Author's collection)*

Bird route; and the other, Holliday & Bangs Ltd of Tulse Hill, started a service from Brixton to Kings Lynn via Chelmsford, Bury St. Edmunds and Swaffham (where they added a branch to Fakenham). They also ran buses in London with the fleetname *Imperial* but the coach service was *Limited Stop Pullman*.

Despite all this, the Corona service held its own. On 1 April 1930 the London departure was reinstated, after what seems to have been a winter withdrawal. A 9.00am journey left Charing Cross and returned at 4.00pm from Stowmarket. (Corona was the only one of the Essex and Suffolk operators to permanently outstation in London). The timings thus established – the other coach left Stowmarket at 7.30am and returned from London at 6.00pm – remained unchanged until the war years. Day-return passengers thus had over six hours in London, while at the other end of the route they could have two-and-a-half hours for shopping in Stowmarket. What was more, the passenger to Sudbury could now arrive from the villages at 8.52am and return at 12.10pm, offering yet another shopping facility.

By this time it was common knowledge in the trade that an Act of Parliament was about to introduce the licensing of bus and coach services and that those who were already running would be able to claim 'grandfather rights'. Many new services were put on at this time, not all of which survived the licensing procedure when it commenced in March 1931. The Corona coaches must have been flourishing by now, requiring the small coaches of the day to be duplicated at busy times. Mr. Chinery's preparation for the new era of licensing was to introduce two feeder services, one from Hadleigh and the other from Hartest, converging on Sudbury. The feeder coaches could then work through to London (or points short) at busy periods and otherwise they could be taken empty to Acton for fuelling and maintenance, which was to become standard practice.

The choice of the feeder routes is explained by reference to the   . At Hadleigh the local branch line departed in the opposite direction to London and passengers then had to change at Bentley, a minor station on the Great Eastern main line, in order to complete their journey. The coach was a clear improvement and sealed the fate of a branch whose local traffic to Ipswich had already been largely lost to Skinner and the Eastern Counties company – the passenger service was withdrawn on 29 February 1932. On the other side of Sudbury, Hartest was a small village from which to run to London and the route took the coach through narrow lanes, touching only the outskirts of Stanstead, but it did include the more substantial village of Glemsford. From January 1924 to March 1927 (I owe the accuracy of this to Eric Axten's records), the National Omnibus & Transport Company had served the route so it seems possible that their abandonment of the route may have influenced Mr. Chinery's choice. This was as far as expansion was feasible to the west, for the next village up the Stour Valley, Cavendish, was already served by Jennings and north of Hartest lay largely empty country.

The leaflets introducing the Hadleigh and Hartest services carried the proviso, "Subject to any order made by the Traffic Commissioners directing otherwise", but, as things turned out, this was not to be a problem. The Corona licence applications took pride of place in the 'Notices and Proceedings' of the Metropolitan Traffic Area and in due course they were among the first to be heard by Sir Haviland Hiley, in the Eastern Area Traffic Court at Cambridge.

The services did not escape unscathed. All intermediate fares within the Metropolitan Area were deleted, while the same pruning in the Eastern Area left the last picking up point for London at Braintree, with intermediate fares to Chelmsford, Brentwood and Romford. The officials at Cambridge were,

however, somewhat troubled by the fact that the service was intended to cater for local traffic over the country end of the route, which made it difficult for them to classify it as either 'stage' or 'express'. This had important consequences, since the average speed allowed on a stage carriage service was lower than that for express, but on the other hand, to divide the route into two would mean that, technically, through bookings could not be made for long-distance journeys. At a much later period the *Grey Pullman* – later Premier Travel – service was in fact truncated at Saffron Walden for licensing purposes, with through fares endorsed on the licence but, in the Corona application, the decision was made to give the service overlapping licences, express from Stowmarket to London, with a stage licence on the same timings from Stowmarket to Sudbury. Mr. Chinery had to withdraw his original applications and replace them and what the decisions did for the statistical records is not recorded, although it probably accounts for the disapproval shown in later years, when the system lent itself to further adjustment.

The two feeder services were licensed, on the assumption that they always ran through to London in each case, which must have distorted the statistics still more. The local service between Acton and Sudbury was also approved, as was an express carriage service between Sudbury and Ipswich, running on Tuesdays only (Ipswich market day) through a number of villages that lay on the main service route. This had originated with a Mr. A. (Pat) Brown, who had established himself with one bus, based at Great Cornard, just south of Sudbury. When licensing was introduced he applied for Sudbury-Bury St. Edmunds, Sudbury-Ipswich, Sudbury–Bulmer Street and Sudbury–Long Melford, each of them on different days. The story then has it that his bus was inspected by a Ministry official one Wednesday as it stood on Chequer Square at Bury and found to be some inches too wide for the Construction and Use Regulations. Presented with a suspension order, it seems that Mr. Brown arranged for Theobald's bus to take his passengers home, left his own where it was and – in the best English tradition – went to sea. His other services covered routes already operated by existing operators, so there was no-one to seek the licences, but the Ipswich route, passing the Corona depot, was different. The exact circumstances of the take-over are not recorded, though it seems no payment could have been made and so Mr. Chinery acquired another service despite the fact that it coincided quite largely with an Eastern Counties route.

In 1931, therefore, the Corona services and their licence numbers, were as shown in **Table Four**.

TABLE FOUR:
Corona services as licensed in 1931

16/4	Acton and Sudbury (stage) - Thursdays and Saturdays
16/6	Excursions and Tours from Sudbury, Long Melford, Acton, Great and Little Waldingfield and Lavenham, mainly to East Coast seaside resorts during the summer months.
16/7	Stowmarket and London (express) - daily
16/8	Hartest and London (express) - daily
16/9	Hadleigh and London (express) - daily
16/11	Sudbury and Ipswich (express) - Tuesdays
16/12	Stowmarket and Sudbury (stage) - daily

In addition, the road haulage side of the business continued and this was the form that Mr. Chinery's operations were to take for the next ten years. The firm made a name for itself through a good standard of coach and through the contribution of the staff, many of whom had been glad to find work when agricultural employment became a victim of the great depression of farming during the inter-war years. One of the attractions

ABOVE: A rare bird – GV 3289, an AEC 'Q', which only lasted three years in the fleet *(Essex Bus Enthusiasts)*

BELOW: GV 1655, an AEC Regal with Duple 32-seat body, maintained the London service from 1933 to the wartime cutback. *(Author's collection)*

of the London service for Suffolk people to whom London was alien and the trains confusing, was the fact that they knew the driver who would fix up a taxi for them and help them on their way.

On 1 January 1932 the London terminal was moved from Charing Cross Embankment to the new Coach Station at King's Cross and by then a regular pattern of operation had been established. Charley Gilson drove the London-based coach to Stowmarket and back and Harry Pleasants (known to everyone as 'Jokey'), who lived at Monks Eleigh, took the other coach from Stowmarket to London and back. One of the Acton men, often Bill Sandford ('Snigley'), would go to London to cover rest-days and holidays, which made rest-day cover expensive, involving two nights away. Ratcliffe, the conductor, lived at Stowmarket and his regular duty was to go up with Jokey to the *White Horse* at Widford (just beyond Chelmsford), where the coaches called for refreshments. He then picked up Gilson's coach and worked back to Stowmarket, where the two men had lunch and he then repeated the morning journeys.

On normal days this gave ample opportunity for all fares to be collected, but could be a bit of a rush at holiday times, when there were duplicates running. The conductor's rest days were covered by one of the Acton drivers, who similarly replaced the Hartest and Hadleigh drivers, each of whom normally kept his vehicle at home (a small shed was rented for the Hartest coach).

The other men worked on the local services and the summer excursions and the private hire work and took a share in the lorry driving. This became a substantial business, with regular contracts from London for the horsehair factory at Glemsford – typical of what the railways would call 'bad loading traffic' because of its low weight-to-bulk ratio, but quite suited for road transport. There were contracts with Stafford Allen too and for the various light industries in Sudbury. Judged by its vehicle policy, the business flourished. Only new vehicles were bought and in 1935 there appeared an example of that rare breed, the AEC 'Q', with its side mounted engine. Judging by the number of pictures that survive, No.19 was the pride of the fleet – an AEC Regal with 32 seats and a centre entrance, such as was to be found in the post-war Regal IV. The Regal and the 'Q' were the biggest coaches in the pre-war fleet, a new Bedford WTB 20-seater being bought as late as 1937 (a 20-seater in those days did not require a conductor when being used on stage carriage services). Not all of the coaches stayed long with the fleet, the 'Q' being sold to Cooper of Combes after just less than three years in service, but No.19 lasted from 1933 until it was sold to Ashdown in Danbury at the beginning of 1941. One pre-war coach broke new ground in being fitted with radio - reputedly the first in the area. It may have been better suited to private hire work than to service operation, where a radio can cause contention among the passengers.

The pre-war days saw very little further changes in the services. A timetable of the early 1930s speaks of 'Latest Type Luxury Coaches', Specially Heated for Winter Travel. Rugs provided' and invites customers to 'Post this to your friends in London'. The timing point in Sudbury was by then shown as 'Sidnell's, North Street' this being the name of the tobacconist that was to be the Sudbury booking agent for many years. The excursion licence acquired new destinations, some for away matches of the Football Club and one for the Essex Show. Rumours of European war must have seemed very far away.

When the war did come there was at first little difference. While the Ministry ordered the suspension of express coach services over most of the country, it was recognised that some had become essential parts of the transport networks and these were allowed to continue - the best-known example was that of the *Royal Blue* services in the West of England, which became a sort of long-distance bus network within that part of the country, shorn of their extensions to London and the Midlands. The Corona service continued first unchanged. The drivers had some unpleasant experiences in the blitz, not least the lorry drivers - horse-hair is very inflammable cargo to be carrying through a firebomb raid. Finally, however, it was decided that the fuel situation did not justify the through route to London and from 2 July 1942 the coaches were turned at Chelmsford Station, connecting there with the London trains.

The London outstation was closed and the service was limited to one journey from Stowmarket at 11am, returning from Chelmsford at 3.30pm, on weekdays except Wednesdays (when there was no service), with a midday journey from Sudbury to Stowmarket and back on Saturdays. A Sunday journey left Stowmarket at 3pm and returned from Chelmsford

at 6pm, except between mid-October and mid-February, when each journey ran earlier, in the darker evenings.

The Hartest feeder service was abandoned for the duration (and after), while Hadleigh connections were provided to the Chelmsford journeys. On this reduced basis, Mr. Chinery continued to trade, helped also by the goods traffic, which towards the end of the war included tipper work on the construction of Waldingfield RAF station (which was being built for the United States Air Force).

The Boom Years

Post-war years saw one major change, when the road haulage side of the business was acquired by British Road Services under the compulsory powers of the Transport Act, 1947. The full London service was reinstated, except for the Hartest feeder, but with significant changes to the timetable, as shown in **Table Five**.

TABLE FIVE: Pre-war and Post-war Timetables					
	Pre-war		Post-war		
	Daily		Mon.-Sat		Sundays
	am	p.m.	am	p.m.	am	p.m.
STOWMARKET	7.30	4.00	8.30	2.15	8.30	8.30
SUDBURY	8.53	5.23	9.53	3.38	9.53	4.53
LONDON	11.44	8.14	12.53	6.38	12.53	7.53
LONDON	9.00	6.00	9.00	2.00	9.00	4.30
SUDBURY	12.10	9.05	12.00	5.00	12.00	7.30
STOWMARKET	1.13	10.13	1.22	6.22	1.22	8.52
Hadleigh timings in each case as appropriate						

These revisions produced considerable saving in labour costs, but they removed the day return facility to London and made weekend passengers (of whom there were many) leave earlier to get home. Local traffic gained, however, by improving the timing of the morning journey into Sudbury and adding a convenient shopping facility in the afternoons, (at the cost of a reasonable facility at the Stowmarket end of the route). Another consequence was that Ratcliffe now had to leave the up coach at Braintree so as to pick up the down service on most journeys.

The post-war years were a boom period for rural bus operators, when food was still rationed and 'austerity' ruled. Travel was one thing people could indulge in; there was plenty of work; and the 1944 Education Act was offering country chil-

LEFT: The first new coach after the war, AGV 696, a Leyland PS1/1 with 32-seat Strachan body, stands outside the running sheds at Acton, with a pre-war Leyland looking a bit shabby at the side. *(Author's collection)*

THE "CORONA COACHES."

Stowmarket—Sudbury—Chelmsford Services

Commencing 2nd July, 1942.

Coach. Depart:	Week-days except Weds.	SUNDAYS ONLY Sats. only.	"Summer"	"Winter"
	A.M.	P.M.	P.M.	P.M.
Stowmarket	10 0	2 0	3 0	1 15
Finborough	10 9	2 9	3 9	1 24
Hitcham	10 21	2 21	3 21	1 36
Bildeston	10 27	2 27	3 27	1 42
Chelsworth	10 32	2 32	3 32	1 47
Monks Eleigh	10 36	2 36	3 36	1 51
Brent Eleigh	10 42	2 42	3 42	1 57
Lavenham	10 50	2 50	3 50	2 5
Waldingfields	10 59	2 59	3 59	2 14
Acton	11 5	3 5	4 5	2 20
Long Melford	11 12	3 12	4 12	2 27
Sudbury	11 23	3 23	4 23	2 38
Halstead	11 36		4 36	2 51
Halstead	11 46		4 46	3 1
Braintree	12 4		5 4	3 19
Chelmsford, arrive	12 33		5 33	3 48
Train.				
Depart Chelmsford	12 45		5 59	4 3
Arrive London	1 35		6 50	4 50
Train.	P.M.			P.M.
Depart London	2 15		5 0	4 0
Arrive Chelmsford	3 16		5 50	4 52
Coach.				
Depart Chelmsford	3 30		6 0	5 0
Braintree	3 59		6 29	5 29
Halstead	4 17		6 47	5 47
Maplestead	4 27		6 57	5 57
Sudbury	4 40		7 10	6 10
Long Melford	4 51	12 0	7 21	6 21
Acton	4 57	12 11	7 27	6 27
Waldingfields	5 3	12 17	7 33	6 33
Lavenham	5 12	12 23	7 42	6 42
Brent Eleigh	5 20	12 32	7 50	6 50
Monks Eleigh	5 26	12 40	7 56	6 56
Chelsworth	5 30	12 46	8 0	7 0
Bildeston	5 35	12 50	8 5	7 5
Hitcham	5 41	12 55	8 11	7 11
Finborough	5 53	1 13	8 23	7 23
Stowmarket, arrive	6 2	1 22	8 32	7 32

WEDNESDAYS — NO SERVICES.

"Winter" Services will operate from the third Sunday in October to the third Sunday in February.

Head Office—Proprietor: **A. CHINERY,** Acton, Sudbury, Suffolk.

Established 1850.   'Phone: Long Melford **200.**

London Service Commenced May, 1929.

Intermediate Fare Table.

Stowmarket—Sudbury—Chelmsford Service

From	To	S.	R.	Pr
CHELMSFORD	BRAINTREE	1/3	2/-	2/-
CHELMSFORD	HALSTEAD	2/-	3/-	3/6
BRAINTREE	HALSTEAD	1/-	1/6	1/6
CHELMSFORD	MAPLESTEAD (Catley Cross)	2/3	3/3	3/9
BRAINTREE	MAPLESTEAD	1/3	2/-	2/-
HALSTEAD	MAPLESTEAD	1/-	1/6	1/6
CHELMSFORD	SUDBURY & LONG MELFORD	2/6	3/6	4/-
BRAINTREE	SUDBURY & LONG MELFORD	1/6	2/6	2/6
HALSTEAD	SUDBURY & LONG MELFORD	1/-	1/6	1/6
CHELMSFORD	ACTON	2/9	4/-	4/6
BRAINTREE	ACTON	1/9	3/-	3/-
HALSTEAD	ACTON	1/3	2/-	2/-
CHELMSFORD	WALDINGFIELDS	2/9	4/-	4/6
BRAINTREE	WALDINGFIELDS	1/9	3/-	3/-
HALSTEAD	WALDINGFIELDS	1/4	2/-	2/-
CHELMSFORD	LAVENHAM	3/-	4/-	5/-
BRAINTREE	LAVENHAM	2/-	3/3	3/3
HALSTEAD	LAVENHAM	1/6	2/6	2/6
CHELMSFORD	BRENT ELEIGH	3/3	4/6	5/6
BRAINTREE	BRENT ELEIGH	2/3	3/6	3/6
HALSTEAD	BRENT ELEIGH	1/6	2/9	2/9
CHELMSFORD	MONKS ELEIGH & CHELSWORTH	3/6	5/-	6/-
BRAINTREE	MONKS ELEIGH & CHELSWORTH	2/6	4/-	4/-
HALSTEAD	MONKS ELEIGH & CHELSWORTH	1/9	3/-	3/-
CHELMSFORD	BILDESTON	3/6	5/-	6/-
BRAINTREE	BILDESTON	2/6	4/-	4/-
HALSTEAD	BILDESTON	2/-	3/6	3/6
CHELMSFORD	HITCHAM	3/9	5/-	6/-
BRAINTREE	HITCHAM	2/9	4/6	4/-
HALSTEAD	HITCHAM	2/3	4/-	4/-
CHELMSFORD	FINBOROUGH	4/-	5/-	6/-
BRAINTREE	FINBOROUGH	2/9	4/-	4/-
HALSTEAD	FINBOROUGH	2/9	4/-	4/-
CHELMSFORD	STOWMARKET	4/-	5/-	6/-
BRAINTREE	STOWMARKET	3/6	5/6	5/6
HALSTEAD	STOWMARKET	3/-	4/6	4/6

Pr denotes Period Return Fares.

Children under 14 Years Half of above Fares.

"CORONA" COACHES.

Hadleigh — Sudbury — Chelmsford Services.

Commencing 2nd July, 1942.

Coach. Depart:	Week Days (except Weds.)	Sundays Only. Summer.	Winter
	A.M.	P.M.	P.M.
Hadleigh	10 40	3 40	1 55
Boxford	11 0	4 0	2 15
Newton	11 10	4 10	2 25
Sudbury	11 23	4 23	2 38
Maplestead	11 36	4 36	2 51
Halstead	11 46	4 46	3 1
Braintree	12 4	5 4	3 19
Chelmsford, arrive	12 33	5 33	3 48
Train.			
Depart Chelmsford	12 45	5 59	4 3
Arrive London	1 35	6 50	4 50
Train.	P.M.		P.M.
Depart London	2 15	5 0	4 0
Arrive Chelmsford	3 16	5 50	4 52
Coach.			
Depart Chelmsford	3 30	6 0	5 0
Braintree	3 59	6 29	5 29
Halstead	4 17	6 47	5 47
Sudbury	4 40	7 10	6 10
Newton	4 50	7 20	6 20
Boxford	5 0	7 30	6 30
Hadleigh, arrive	5 20	7 50	6 50

WEDNESDAYS — NO SERVICES.

"Winter" Services will operate from the third Sunday in October to the third Sunday in February.

Intermediate Fare Table.

From	To	S.	R.	Pr
CHELMSFORD	BRAINTREE	1/3	2/-	2/-
CHELMSFORD	HALSTEAD	2/-	3/-	3/6
BRAINTREE	HALSTEAD	1/-	1/6	1/6
CHELMSFORD	MAPLESTEAD (Catley Cross)	2/3	3/9	3/9
BRAINTREE	MAPLESTEAD	1/3	2/-	2/-
HALSTEAD	MAPLESTEAD	1/-	1/6	1/6
CHELMSFORD	SUDBURY & LONG MELFORD	2/6	3/6	4/-
BRAINTREE	SUDBURY & LONG MELFORD	1/6	2/6	2/6
HALSTEAD	SUDBURY & LONG MELFORD	1/-	1/6	1/6
CHELMSFORD	NEWTON	3/-	4/-	5/-
BRAINTREE	NEWTON	1/9	3/-	3/-
HALSTEAD	NEWTON	1/3	2/-	2/-
CHELMSFORD	BOXFORD	3/-	4/-	5/-
BRAINTREE	BOXFORD	1/9	2/6	3/-
HALSTEAD	BOXFORD	1/4	2/-	2/6
CHELMSFORD	HADLEIGH	3/6	5/-	5/-
BRAINTREE	HADLEIGH	2/3	3/6	3/9
HALSTEAD	HADLEIGH	2/3	3/-	3/-

Pr denotes **PERIOD RETURN FARES.**

Children under 14 years Half of above Fares.

Head Office—Proprietor: **A. CHINERY,**
Acton, Sudbury, Suffolk.

'Phone: Long Melford 1929.

Established 1850.   'Phone: Long Melford **2**

London Service Commenced May, 1929.

14

ABOVE: CCF 463 was the workhorse of the London service throughout the author's period of management, and served faithfully to the end. *(Author's collection)*

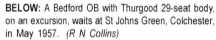

LEFT: CCF 596, one of the two Leylands with Gurney Nutting 35-seat bodies, turns from Barley Lane into High Road, Goodmayes, on Thursday 12 June 1952, at about 6pm. The date matters, for it means the coach was not working the London service, as might be supposed, but it is still a typical Corona operation. *(G D Sharp)*

BELOW: A Bedford OB with Thurgood 29-seat body, on an excursion, waits at St Johns Green, Colchester, in May 1957. *(R N Collins)*

dren the chance of a secondary education, in many cases for the first time. Operators expanded their services to meet the demand, among them being Chambers of Bures, who for the first time came through Acton on a new service to Bury St. Edmunds on Wednesdays and Saturdays. At the same time the Corona services began to expand. On 2 January 1950 the Hartest feeder was restored and on 21 February 1951 a 'picture bus' was put on between Lavenham and Sudbury on Wednesday and Saturday evenings, leaving Sudbury at '10pm or at conclusion of second-house at cinemas'. (This was a typical development in rural transport in the years before television took the traffic away and represented a useful additional source of revenue for a bus that had already 'earned its keep' during the day. The driver got a free evening out in addition to a small overtime payment).

Then it was decided to strengthen the service over the Sudbury - Halstead section, with additional journeys that appeared on the stage carriage licence (in1946 this had been extended to become Stowmarket – Halstead). This section of road had never supported a daily through service for long, largely because the villages lie to either side of it. Eastern National, Blackwell and Harry Rippingale of Gestingthorpe all ran over it on one day or another and all objected (the other operator, Theobald, only ran on Sundays and so had no locus). A rather unsatisfactory grant was made, with serious restrictions on the sections over which traffic could be carried and only one journey that actually ran every weekday. This was introduced on 2 February 1953, but the results were so discouraging that it was reduced to Tuesdays, Fridays and Saturdays only, with effect from 25 July (but with the addition of a picture bus in and out of Halstead on Saturdays). Even this was over-providing and the 'additional service' was reduced to Saturdays only, with effect from 24 April 1954.

There was also public pressure for a return to the pre-war London timings and on 1 September 1952 a number of new journeys were added to the express licence, to meet the demand without basically affecting the schedule for Charley Gilson and Jokey. A 7.30am coach from Stowmarket, with feeder connections, was put on to run on Fridays throughout the year and on Wednesdays from 1 March to the end of October. This coach returned from King's Cross at 6pm, thus giving the day return facility and also allowing weekenders to leave London on Fridays after work – a much-valued improvement. By this time, too, the afternoon up journey on Sundays was requiring duplication every week, so a return trip at 8.15pm from King's Cross was added, to work the relief coach back in traffic (the feeder services only connected with this journey in the summer months). All this had involved further objections and Eastern National succeeded in barring traffic between Halstead, Braintree and London on the additional journeys (except for the Sunday 8.15pm in the winter).

Finally the post-war period of national service had given rise to demand all over the country for leave services from RAF stations and other military camps. For a few years this became a money-spinner for the private coach firms, not all of whom troubled to licence their operations. RAF Wattisham was the only station remotely connected with Corona territory, but there were other firms within reach of it and for some time the Wattisham-London leave coaches were an open market. It was usual for such services to be arranged semi-officially, with tickets on sale in the canteen (sometimes the PSI acted as agent on a normal commission basis) but it was not uncommon for individual airmen to book a coach and make a small profit by selling seats on it - an illegal practice under the Road Traffic Act. Wattisham saw its share of doubtful practices, leading to a few prosecutions, until eventually the three operators chiefly involved – W. J. Cooper of Combs, near Stowmarket and B. A. Taylor & Sons of Bildeston, along with Corona Coaches – obtained licences allowing them to operate the service in rotation. (Despite this, other operators, notably Mulleys Motorways and Partridge of Layham, continued to carry the airmen).

With the end of the war the fleet could be replaced, again with new vehicles. The first, a Bedford OWB with bus bodywork and 32 seats, came in 1945. Two coaches, an AEC Regal III and a Leyland Tiger PS1/1, came in 1947, but were sold again by 1952, while the first of the vehicles that we were to operate arrived in 1949. The last pre-war coach - the Bedford 20-seater referred to earlier – was sold in 1954, in which year there appeared the first second-hand vehicle to be bought, so far as the records go, in the history of the company: a Bedford OB with Duple *Vista* body, obtained from a London operator. By this time the largest coach was the AEC *Regal IV*, seating 41 passengers, which became the pride of the fleet and was pictured on the timetable leaflets.

This then was the Corona business when Bert Davidson and I were looking at it with an eye to purchase. Fares had risen - by 1954 Sudbury-London was 6/9 (34p) single, 9/3 (46p) day return and 12/- (60p) period return. There were 11 coaches, all of them post-war, in the distinctive chocolate and tangerine livery that Mr. and Mrs. Chinery had chosen for Corona. Seven drivers and one conductor were supplemented by part-timers. The nerve centre of the business was still the depot at Acton, where Mr. Chinery was assisted in the management of the firm by Len Hazell, who kept the books and made out the daily orders for the men, but in the early '50s a house called "Wisteria Cottage" had been acquired in Sudbury and this had become the registered office of Corona Coaches Ltd, the company formed by Mr. and Mrs. Chinery in 1946.

Here the booking office was presided over by Maude Swindells, whose husband, Bill, was one of the longest serving members of staff and was regarded as senior driver. The house stood at the junction of East Street and North Street (later it was occupied by a wine merchant), at a point then known as Old Market Place. The garden in front had been cleared and levelled (with the loss of a fine chestnut), to provide hard standing for two coaches and the Sudbury timing point had been moved to what was in effect a small coach station (only the Lavenham picture buses and the extra Halstead journeys used the Market Hill bus stands). Display cases for posters were installed and Corona was now firmly part of the Sudbury scene – a business rooted in the communities that it served.

Chapter Three

DREAM AND REALITY

A gleam in the eye

I count myself fortunate in having been given two years to study the subject that interested me most, but the life of a post graduate student at the LSE in the 1950s was not madly exciting. In term time I went to the School about twice a week for my lectures and for the postgraduate seminar and most of the work was done at home at Hadstock. With so much time spent in detailed study of the bus industry and in collecting still more data about it, the idea of running my own business came naturally. I don't know when I committed myself to it as an objective but it was before the end of my first year, while I was still unsure whether I would have my studentship renewed.

What I do know is that, step-by-step, the dream crystallized around the company, until it took all my spare attention and threatened to become an obsession. With the help of a few papers that I preserved I can reconstruct the steps as they were taken, and the power that the dream came to hold over me gives me instant total recall even now, so that in my mind's eye I can see a Corona coach disappearing down Friars street in Sudbury as I saw it in 1946, long before it began.

The first step was taken through the Omnibus Society - once again the catalyst in my career. I read a paper on 27 February 1953 called 'Independent Bus Services In West Suffolk', which was printed in the Omnibus Magazine (Vol. XII, No 85). (I now find the conclusion prophetic, so I have reproduced it as Appendix I). The paper was well received and Eric Osborne, with whom I formed a close friendship, suggested that I should organise a study tour of the area. It was a tradition dating back to the formation of the Society to make such tours, thanks to the hospitality of the unnumbered operators, large and small, and the two firms that I chose for the party to visit were Jennings of Ashen and Corona Coaches. On 27 April I went to see the proprietors concerned.

Barney Jennings made me welcome and told me how he had come over from Ireland in the 1920's and set up the business; how he had established the Clare–Thaxted–London service; and how he had chosen deliberately not to expand beyond the size that he could manage well. Hugh Springett, his manager, was equally friendly and helpful - later he succeeded to the business, though still using the Jennings name. At

BELOW: The new team takes over. Left to right: Bert Davidson, Mrs Chinery, John Foley Egginton, Alan Chinery, Alan Phillips, and the author. *(Richard Burn)*

Acton I was made just as welcome - Mr. and Mrs. Chinery talked about Corona and its history and introduced me to their daughter, Rona, who disappointed me by saying she thought all buses should be state owned. The OS visit was approved, and after being shown round the running sheds and the office, I left for home. On the way, somewhere between Long Melford and Glemsford, the dream was born.

It is my habit to rush ahead with a new idea, thinking, 'wouldn't it be wonderful if...' By the time I got home I had been running Corona long enough to realise my own weaknesses in that respect – however good my traffic sense was, at 27, I lacked business experience and had little knowledge of motor engineering. And I had worked out what to do about it. When I got home and told my wife I don't think she believed it could ever happen but within a month I was in Birmingham, talking to Bert Davidson about a partnership.

I had met Bert – yet again, through the Omnibus Society - when I was a student in Birmingham. The late Peter Hardy invited me to go with the Midland branch to visit the Stratford Blue Company and the coach we used was hired from Allenways, of which Bert was Managing Director. He decided to join the party and when he and I got talking we found we had both been at the Grammar School in Colchester. After that we kept in touch and when I was with Premier Travel I introduced him to Arthur Lainson. As a result, Premier bought the Birmingham–Harwich service from Allenways and the terminal of Service 5 (Clacton-Birmingham) was moved to the Allenways coach station in Park street.

Bert's ideas for the future of Allenways did not altogether agree with those of his co-directors and at about the time I left Premier he resigned and took a job as Manager of Kendrick's Coaches at Dudley. I knew he regarded this as an interim

BELOW: May 1958 timetable leaflet showing express coach services

Travel Corona

MAIN BOOKING AGENTS

LONDON King's Cross Coach Station, Pentonville Road, N.1., or any P.S.V. Agent in London or the Home Counties
CHELMSFORD Rose Bros. Ltd., 66a Duke Street
Messrs. T. Rippon & Sons, 11 High Street
BRAINTREE Mr. Rudkin 11 Manor Street
HALSTEAD Mr. Nice, 69 High Street
LT. MAPLESTEAD Mrs. Jelley, The Post Office
TWINSTEAD Mrs. McCracken, The Wagon and Horses
WICKHAM ST. PAUL Mrs. Harding, The Stores
GESTINGTHORPE Mr. Hollingsworth, The Stores
BELCHAMP WALTER Mr. J. Finch
BULMER TYE Mr. Stott, The Post Office
LONG MELFORD Mr. Blythe, Fruiterer, Hall Street
FOXEARTH Mrs. Ham, The Post Office
GT. WALDINGFIELD Mr. Heard, The Post Office
LT. WALDINGFIELD Mr. Horsley, The Stores
LAVENHAM Mr. Fisk, Fruiterer, 2 Church Street
BRENT ELEIGH Mrs. Elmer, The Post Office
MONKS ELEIGH Mr. Caton, The Post Office
CHELSWORTH Mr. Whymark, The Peacock
BILDESTON Messrs. K. and I. Self, Stationers, 82/4 High Street
HITCHAM Mr. Goody, The Post Office
FINBOROUGH Mr. Mortimer, The Post Office
STOWMARKET Messrs. O. G. Barnard and Sons Ltd , Station Rd.
Messrs. Durrants. 12 Ipswich Street
HADLEIGH Mr. Bloomfield, Newsagent, 35 High Street
BOXFORD Mr. Riddlestone, Newsagent, Swan Street
GLEMSFORD Mr. Baines, The Post Office
STANSTEAD Messrs. E. and W. C. Ringer, The Post Office
HARTEST Miss Redgrave, The Post Office
BROCKLEY Mr. White, The Post Office
REDE Mr Miller, The Stores
BURY ST. EDMUNDS Messrs. Fairtax (Travel) Ltd. Brentgovel Street

The Gateway to West Suffolk

IF IT'S TRAVEL CORONA WILL HELP YOU

CORONA COACHES LTD.

OLD MARKET PLACE
SUDBURY, SUFFOLK
Telephone : SUDBURY 2193

TIME TABLES
OF
EXPRESS COACH SERVICES

LONDON
AND
SUDBURY — LAVENHAM
HADLEIGH — HARTEST
STOWMARKET

FROM 19th MAY 1958 UNTIL FURTHER NOTICE
Book with

Printed by Bayley's Printers Limited, Ipswich

E5 /58/60

ABOVE: Around the time when we took over the business, Senior Driver Bill Swindells reflects on the new situation. *(Dawn King)*

position, for like me his heart was in service operation rather than excursions and contract hire. He had started on the freight side, with John Morton of Coventry, but his interest was in passenger work and I knew he was a good organiser – I had been impressed with the booking and accounting system he had set up at Allenways as well as with his engineering knowledge.

On 21 May 1953 I saw Bert at his home in Acocks Green and met his wife Ena and the two girls. The idea of the partnership attracted him from the first and we agreed to go ahead. I would give him all the data I had and he would start working out the sort of price we could offer. I had a bit of capital; Bert was willing to sell his house and put the proceeds into the kitty; the rest we would have to borrow. The dream was becoming a business reality. I said I thought my wife would approve; Bert said that Ena would 'up sticks and follow him without question'.

Meantime the OS tour was going ahead. I hired a 33-seat Leyland Tiger from Premier and on Sunday, 7 June it left King's Cross on a perfect summers day, with God's own country looking its best. (Whether by that I mean Suffolk or Essex is irrelevant – for me it's both). We followed every twist and turn of the Jennings route, passing through Thaxted and Finchingfield till we reached the garage at Ashen - converted from the village school. There the two Leyland Olympians (one the prototype) were posed for the cameras – rare birds indeed for a small rural operator, with integral construction well ahead of their time. After that we followed the rest of the route to Clare and then stopped for lunch at the Cherry Tree at Stradishall.

After lunch we cut across to Stansfield, where we joined Long's Clare–Bury St. Edmunds route, which was later to become Corona's. At Bury we were joined by C. S. V. Taylor on Angel Hill, an OS member from Thetford, who explained the many independent services that entered the town and then we turned south over Chambers' route to Lavenham, where we stopped again. Lavenham on a summers day must stir the heart of any Englishman and here was the countryside I hoped to live in and serve. I had a full heart as we pulled into Acton, not far ahead of the London service.

The Chinery family made the party welcome, flattered a bit, perhaps, by the interest taken in their business by all these people. The London coaches came through – Charley Gilson driving the service car, with (I think) Bill Sandford on a relief from Bildeston, scheduled to work the 8.15pm back from King's Cross. I stood aside from the crowd, taking it all in, feeling already a deep sense of possession, as if this were somehow my world. It was more than just the business now; more than the vehicles or the timetables; it was the people and the place. Not just Acton but Suffolk and Essex - 'the land, the work and the folk', as Frédérick le Play put it, whose work I had studied at the Institute of Sociology. Here, it seemed to me, I would find the satisfactions that had eluded me for so long. From then on I wanted very much to run Corona.

When the coaches had left, we took the direct lane to Sudbury so as to get there before them. At the Old Market Place we met Len Hazell, the Manager and watched the Hartest passengers transfer; the Hadleigh car was to work through as far as Chelmsford and then return as a relief to the 4.30pm from London - normal practice on all but the quietest Sundays. Eventually all was peaceful again, with the Hartest coach parked up on the forecourt, waiting for the next arrival and we were shown around the office. Great admiration was shown for Rona Chinery's Coronation poster and also for the picture of the AEC 'Q' of pre-war days. Finally we went to the Priory Gate Hotel, where the Chinery's were guests of the Society for tea, before the Premier coach took the party home.

Negotiations proceeding

The next six months saw little development, unless it was in my mind and Bert's. I had an interview at LSE – at a high level: Sir Arnold Plant and Michael Oakeshott as well as Gilbert Ponsonby – which decided my immediate future. My studentship was renewed and I was allowed to register for my MSc. The Coronation came and went but it seemed an event in the background. Whatever preoccupied me in my personal life, the thought of running Corona and its possibilities remained the underlying theme.

Bert did his sums and came up with the following estimate of what the business was worth:

Vehicles and plant	£17,070 *	
Less Hire Purchase commitment	5,770	£11,300
Estimate for goodwill		3,000
Estimate for property		4,000
* see table 00		

We reckoned we could find more than half of this. When my grandfather died in 1941 he left his estate in trust for the benefit of his widow during her lifetime, after which I had the reversion of a substantial sum. I talked to George Gilbert, the family solicitor, who told me that I could borrow on this expectation. My mother who had recently come into a legacy from an uncle in Australia offered to put something into the business too. Bert, as I have said, was willing to put in the proceeds of selling his house on the understanding that he lived in the company's house at Acton rent-free on a service tenancy. At first I expected to live in the house at Sudbury but my wife would not agree, so I refrained from committing the value of my house at Hadstock. All the same, interest rates were still low and we calculated that we could repay our net borrowing over 18 years or thereabouts. I was 28 and Bert 39, so we were young enough to have a reasonable chance of seeing the business free of debt. At the end of the day we would have capitalized our own efforts and in the meantime we would have independence and a living doing what we enjoyed most. It must have been in September 1953, at the time of the Omnibus Society visit to Midland Red, that we sat and worked this out and I began to feel that the dream was within reach. From then on, I was determined to achieve it.

The new term kept me busy, with a thesis to prepare but there was also the matter of my employment when my studentship ended in the following year. Arthur Lainson suggested that I should buy a bus and set up in business with it - Premier would give me inter-hiring work. Gilbert Ponsonby was sympathetic with my wish to go back into management (and had therefore advised me to take a Master's degree and not a Doctorate). He suggested Surrey Motors, the firm owned by Rees Jeffreys himself. I had thoughts of Grey Green or Birch Bros. but my heart was in Corona and by the end of the term I had decided, with Bert's agreement, to start something moving.

On 7 December my wife and I went over to Acton and met the Chinerys again. I had told Alan that I wanted to discuss a matter of business and that evening I raised the possibility of making an offer for Corona, mentioning that I had a partner in the background. His reaction was non-committal but then his reactions generally were. He had the East Anglian humour that understates everything and that outsiders find so difficult to understand. He was a little man and I always remember him wearing a light brown suit and a dark brown felt hat. He used to put the hat on when the telephone rang, for he was never without it, even in the sitting room at Acton. I asked him once, "Gov'nor, why do you always put your hat on to answer the phone?" He said, "That always mean trouble: I've got to go out". Later I was to learn how right he was.

I saw Bert shortly afterwards and we decided to make a formal move. We had agreed that the whole thing was to be a partnership and that the ordinary shares would be held in equal proportion, with the surplus of my own capital held in the form of non-voting preference shares. We would be joint managing directors, Bert being Secretary, with responsibility for finance and engineering, while I took on traffic and day-to-day management. I felt we were as good as there when I wrote to Alan Chinery on 4 January 1954, confirming our interest in the business and asking for financial and commercial information.

The result was an invitation to go to Acton and Bert came to stay at Hadstock so that we could go over together. The occasion was overcast by the reservations that were being expressed by my wife and her family, which reflected a certain middle-class academic dislike of business, that seems to me to account for so much of the failure of the British economy. But we went over on 5 February and Bert was able to see for himself what the business looked like. We obtained little hard data, though – the company's year ended on 31 October and the 1953 balance sheet was not ready. It was with a sense of anticlimax that I saw Bert off to Birmingham and got on with my own work.

I saw him again a month later, when we took stock of things. We agreed we would need professional advice and I said I would have a word with Eric Osborne and see if there was an accountant in the Omnibus Society who would be able

to help us: someone with a feel for the industry. Bert introduced me to John Foley Eggiton, a well known Birmingham solicitor, who was to prove a great support and mentor to us, and a result of that was that we both became early members of the Institute of Traffic Administration, which John had been involved in founding. He confirmed that we were on the right lines in our calculations and so did Douglas Spray, the OS colleague whom Eric suggested and who was to become a better friend than we knew.

In due course we were told that the accounts had been prepared and Douglas and I went over to Acton to see them on 21 May. From what we then saw, it seemed that we had tended to over-value the business but that we were on the right lines. It seemed in a reasonably healthy state but was making very little return on its capital. We heartened ourselves with the thought that there would be scope for improvement and started looking for sources of additional investment.

Suddenly nothing happened. I kept in touch – on 13 June, Derek Giles and I organized another study tour for the Omnibus Society, this time looking at Essex operators, with a memorable visit to Moore's of Kelvedon and we hired a Bedford Vega from Corona. On 29 June, Alan Chinery came to Hadstock, where he was more non-committal than ever as we returned his hospitality. Not that this was surprising: what we did not know was that he was negotiating with Grey Green and had also spoken to Jack Mulley and A. S. Braybrooke of Mendlesham, two sizeable operators, who considered a joint purchase. (I was to learn all this much later, when I was working for Jack). In July, though, an old friend of mine, with whom my wife and I had been staying, suggested that he would be willing to invest in the project, which kept my spirits up remarkably.

By the end of that summer term the thesis was by no means complete and, as I have already said, Gilbert Ponsonby found me a source of income in researching for John Whitbread. If the thesis had been finished I would have had to look for a permanent job in the summer of 1954; instead, the Corona project came to life again, with a letter in August from the company's accountants: Bland, Fielden of Colchester; saying that their client was willing to receive an offer. (The Blands, of course, had been at the Grammar School in both Bert's days and my own, so, we were on home ground, as it were). From what Jack told me, I gather that no offer was forthcoming from Grey Green and since his daughter (now married to a farmer) did not want the business, Alan Chinery, at the age of 59, decided to retire.

We decided to box clever. Knowing that the company's year was coming to an end, we said we would like to wait until we could have sight of the 1954 accounts. Why it is that accountants take so long to do these things I shall never understand but it was to be March 1955 before we received them.

Throughout that period of limbo, I clung more strongly than ever to the hope of success and committed more and more of my emotions to the Corona dream with every month that passed. In September Bert and I went to the Commercial Motor Show at Earls Court and he suggested we approach Eric Osborne to take a stake in the company and become our chairman. There might be times, he said, when we would need someone to resolve any differences that might arise. Eric agreed – like so many enthusiasts, he had always wanted to be involved in running a bus company, while of course there were mutual benefits to be obtained from his profession as an insurance broker.

My son, Michael, was born in the November and this, with various personal involvements, occupied much of my time. I wonder today how I managed to find enough to live on but I made no attempt to find a permanent job, so determined was I that the Corona project would succeed. In March 1955 we received the accounts from Bland, Fielden and things began to move again.

I had already arranged to stay with Bert when I went to speak to the Midland Branch of the Omnibus Society on 16 March. We looked over the figures and amended the original calculations as follows:

Vehicles and plant	£15,850		
Less Hire Purchase			
commitment	2,700	£13,150	
Less sundry items		2,100	11,050
Estimate for goodwill			2,000
			£13,050

These figures do not allow for property but, if this is added at our original estimate of £4,000, the outcome is £17,050, which is about £1,000 less than our previous figure (those were non-inflationary times). We decided to work on this basis and a meeting was arranged at Colchester for 21 April. (Four days earlier I had the odd experience of seeing Alan Chinery and the new Vega, GGV 823, at the first Coach Rally at Clacton-on-Sea, which I attended with the Premier Travel party – it seemed better not to speak to the Corona people).

The additional capital requirement now became pressing and I saw my friend twice, once alone and once with Bert. His offer was generous and went a long way to meeting our needs and he was willing to take shares in the company as the sole collateral. Mother renewed her offer and her wish to see me established in my own business if that was 'what I wanted.' We went to Bland, Fielden's chambers in Sir Isaacs Walk feeling that we were about to settle our future.

It was not to be. Round the table there were seven people; Mr. and Mrs. Chinery and Mr. Digby, their accountant; Eric, Bert and myself, with Douglas as our financial advisor. We made our offer and it seems strange to me now that I have no record of what it was. I remember argument over detail and the realisation that we none of us knew just how much Alan Chinery had heard, when he happened to mention that he had switched his hearing aid off so as to think about one of our points! The meeting broke up with nothing decided and a few days later we had a letter from Bland, Fielden, saying that the difference between our offer and their client's valuation of the business was so great that no purpose could be served by continuing the negotiations.

Bert and I went to see John Foley Egginton. We did not feel inclined even then to abandon hope. It had turned out that Mr. Chinery put a value of £18,000 on the business, plus another £5,000 for goodwill – without including the property. This was some £2,000 above our calculation but we felt we could go a bit further and wrote back to make a revised offer of £20,000 for the business (without property), 'Less £5,000 in respect of hire purchase commitments; and the excess of liabilities over assets.

John continued to express his confidence in our potential aspirants in partnership and so did Eric. At John's suggestion, we placed an advertisement in Commercial Motor, giving his address and inviting information about bus and coach businesses that might be for sale. I must admit I was less than enthusiastic, for my heart was in the Corona dream but the advice was sensible, even though the results were disappointing. Most of the responses – there were only seven – came from firms with no regular services and the only one that was at all

possible came from Mr. C. Gresswell, of Billingborough, near Sleaford. Bert was interested but I felt that his little group of services (listed in Table Seven) would hardly support both of us and would in any case be very dull to manage, with little chance of further development. The thought of life in the Lincolnshire flatlands did not attract me either; it was

TABLE SEVEN:
Cresswell's services

Aslackby and Spalding	- - - -	Tuesdays only
Aslackby and Boston	- - - -	Wednesdays & Saturdays
Aslackby and Bourne	- - - -	Thursdays only
Sleaford and Bourne	- - - -	Daily
Aslackby and Skegness	- - - -	seasonal express

no substitute for Suffolk (and it put my wife off entirely). John agreed and we decided to have one more go at Bland, Fielden, when there had been no reply for over a month. We wrote again and in July we heard that their clients, while unable to accept our offer, felt that a further meeting would be profitable. On 21 July it took place, this time in Sudbury and this time our fate was sealed.

My memory of this meeting is even weaker than that of the previous one and I am not even sure where it took place. I think I was getting desperate – it was three years now since I had worked full-time for a salary and for the past twelve months my income had been sketchy to say the least. My part-time bus conducting had brought in enough to pay the mortgage and find the housekeeping, leaving me time to sell articles where I could to make up the balance but with a new baby we did not have a lot to live on: and to start looking for a job would mean waiting even longer than I then thought possible.

Bert was equally determined and I came to depend very much upon his calculations of what would be feasible. If I had done the sums myself I *might* have said, "No, this is too much", but I accepted his judgement and we made an offer which went above what we had intended. The property was to be transferred at valuation, on a mortgage from Alan Chinery, which reduced our capital needs but placed a further burden on our ability to service any loans we might need; the stock of spares was to be paid for at a price to be agreed upon.

It was with a sense of relief tinged with doubt that I walked up Market Hill, feeling that soon this would be 'my place'. The doubt was reinforced when a letter came from Douglas, saying that he thought we had over-stretched ourselves and that he could no longer act on our behalf. He felt that we were offering more than the business was worth. Neither Eric nor Bert went along with this, though, and I agreed with them that it would be up to us to develop sufficient traffic to make it pay. I had enough confidence in myself to believe we could, and soon Eric came up with an introduction to a firm of London accountants, just building up their practice, who offered us a loophole.

SCHEDULE OF TAKINGS
1955 - 1956

Takings for the period		
1 November 1955 to 31 January 1956:		£4,109. 10s. 1d
Takings for the period		
1 February 1956 to 31 October 1956:		
Contract Hire	£1,079.12s. 9d	
Express Services	£12,771. 6s. 2d	
Luggage charges	£61.13s. 6d	
Stage fares	£ 1,851. 3s. 11d	
Tours	£1,094.12s. 3d	
Private hire	£1,846.16s 9d	£ 19,705. 5s. 4d
Total takings for year ended		
31 October 1956:		**£22,814.15s. 5d**

This was in essence a tax-avoidance scheme. Bert liked the sound of it and the details were worked out at the accountants' offices off Portland Place. It involved forming a second company, which would acquire the vehicles and lease them to Corona Coaches. This company we called Corona Motor Services and we then formed a third company, Corona Holdings, whose shares we actually owned. I think we all got a little innocent pleasure out of feeling what crafty financiers we were, and Bert and Eric got to speaking about 'the Corona Group' but it did not add up to much when it came to running the business. What really mattered was that the Inland Revenue accepted it and it made the scheme feasible, even if it didn't guarantee that it would be viable.

The new accountants, like everyone else, seemed to have every confidence in Bert and me as businessmen. I had every confidence in myself as a traffic manager and Bert felt the same about his abilities on the financial side. So we pushed and scraped and did all we could to tie the deal up. The process was still to be slow.

John went to work on the agreement for sale, with Alan Phillips, the solicitor for the company (whose subsequent friendship has been for me one of the truly good things to come out of it all). By the time the first provisional completion date –1 November 1955 – had been reached, we still had not got our finances together and it was postponed for a month. Then in November there was a third meeting, in London this time, at which Alan Chinery agreed to leave £7,500 to be repaid, with interest, over ten years – a decision

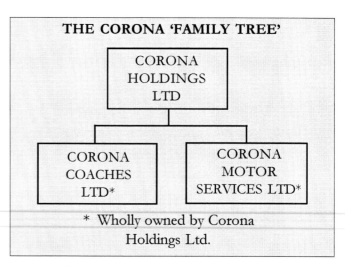

THE CORONA 'FAMILY TREE'

CORONA HOLDINGS LTD

CORONA COACHES LTD*

CORONA MOTOR SERVICES LTD*

* Wholly owned by Corona Holdings Ltd.

that meant further delay but represented yet another expression of confidence in our ability. All of this of course had to be explained to our sleeping partner, which meant another trip to meet him at Ely and of course I had to keep my mother informed because of her similar involvement.

When the December deadline had to be abandoned we decided not to attempt a takeover in the middle of the holiday season and the new date was set for 1 February 1956. After the best part of three years, my dream was to become reality. I realised that I had no idea what that reality was going to be like.

Chapter Four

THE DREAM COMES TRUE

Finding Things Out

On 31 January 1956 the entire staff of Corona Coaches, with the old and the new directors, sat down to dinner in Sudbury at the invitation of Mr. & Mrs. Chinery. John Foley Egginton and Alan Phillips, the two Solicitors, were with us, and I know I felt very nervous and uncertain. I had been away by myself for a few days, staying at the "Swan" at Bibury, in Gloucestershire, to try and sort my ideas out and do some thinking while walking in the Cotswolds, but it hadn't helped much and I faced the future ill-prepared, although I wouldn't admit it even to myself. Bert stayed at Hadstock for a few days, until he could move his family into Corona House at Acton and on the first morning as we drove over he said, "You'll probably need to lean on me a good bit at first". Though I didn't like to admit that need, it was in fact true. What helped both of us most of all, though, was the enormous goodwill that the staff showed towards us from the first.

Next to Corona House stood the office; a wooden hut with high, sloping, desks at which one sat on stools in nineteenth century splendour. Behind the office was the workshop, while across the road the running sheds had been built in a large field. At the entry to the yard in front of the sheds was a small hut where lubricants were stored and the fuel tanks and pumps. (We had hopes of increasing our income by opening a public filling station there, but the petrol company reckoned that the

sales potential was too small). Beside the yard and dominating the scene, stood the 'Crown', whose public bar served as a rest-room for off-duty staff. For a while, this group of buildings was the centre of our activities.

Bert had a PSV driving licence, which I had failed to achieve, but we agreed that it would be best if I did not try again and stuck to conducting. One of us, after all, had to stay and mind the shop. We both of us quickly took our turn on the coaches, though and began to collect the information we needed to make our management effective. Bert had to spend hours with Mr. Chinery, valueing the stock of spares, a great part of which turned out to be obsolete, so that we found we had to spend money to little purpose and paid roughly £1,000 more than our estimate. He also had to report the poor state of the tyres – we had inherited an ill-shod fleet. On the other hand, we were intrigued to discover an agreement with the Transport and General Workers Union, which lay in a drawer. It set out a very reasonable basis for the drivers' pay, but it carried no signature. This it seemed was well known to Billy Bird, our shop steward and turned out to be to everyone's advantage. It kept the local TGWU official off our back, since he could always report to Transport House that the Corona was organised, while at the same time, so long as we respected it in normal practice, we could easily depart from it by mutual agreement when special circumstances arose.

BELOW: The staff dinner on the eve of the change of ownership. *(Richard Burn)*

23

THIS PAGE
LEFT: The Hartest and Hadleigh feeder coaches waiting for the 9 am from Kings Cross to reach Sudbury. *(B Knowlman)*

BELOW: The London coach arrives: it is 12 noon and passengers are waiting to fill the seats as others alight. *(B Knowlman)*

OPPOSITE PAGE
TOP RIGHT: The return journey - Sunday afternoon in Lavenham, and the Regal IV has a good load already. *(B Knowlman)*

LOWER RIGHT: The Regal ready to leave Sudbury, with the feeder coaches and a relief waiting to follow. *(B Knowlman)*

LEFT: DGV 123 on Market Hill, Sudbury, working through from Hadleigh as a London relief (the service car is in the background) in May 1956. We later banned the use of relief on our blinds. *(Frank Church)*

CENTRE: The down London car resting at the refreshment halt at Widford *White Horse,* near Chelmsford. *(Author's collection)*

BOTTOM: ECF 305, an AEC Regal IV and the heaviest coach in the fleet, standing at Old Market Place, Sudbury (probably loading for an excursion) in August 1956. *(Frank Church)*

The fleet was not only run down, it was becoming obsolete. Appendix II lists the vehicles we took over and not one of them was a genuine example of the latest underfloor-engined luxury coach. Even ECF, the Regal IV, was a peculiar monster, not really suited for the work we had to do – it was always awkward to conduct, with its heavy centre door, which needed a certain knack to open or close and was quite beyond the power of many of our passengers to cope with.

ECF was interesting, though, in its transmission: it had a *pre-selective* gearbox, with which only a minority of Regal IVs were then so fitted, apart from London Transport.

You set the next gear you wanted by means of a knob on the steering column and shifted gear when necessary by using a trip pedal on the floor (not unlike the bell trip on a Birmingham tram). This then used compressed air to make the shift – and an expensive piece of equipment was the compressor. Properly used, the box worked well and once it enabled the driver to save the life of a child who ran out in front, by dropping straight down into first. The coach, with its pronounced front overhang, almost dug its nose into the road, but it stopped and the passengers were affected far less than might be expected. On the other hand, drivers need instruction in new equipment and small firms are not always good at this – one of the younger men pointed out to me that most of the staff tended to double de-clutch with the gear trip! (We had trouble, too, in getting them to start away in first gear with the petrol engined coaches).

The three big Bedfords were the only true luxury coaches we owned, but by

26

*The beauty of Britain
lies along her roads*

LAVENHAM, SUFFOLK

By courtesy of East Anglian Magazine

A Day in the Country . . .

Explore the unspoilt villages of East Anglia

The Coach leaves every morning at 9 o'clock from

KINGS CROSS COACH STATION

(also from Stepney, Stratford, Ilford, Romford, Brentwood, Chelmsford)

BOOK YOUR SEAT AT

CORONA COACHES LTD.

THE GATEWAY to WEST SUFFOLK

E4/57/100

This table shows the bookings that can be made by Corona Coaches for day excursions into the countryside of Essex and West Suffolk. Your Booking Agent will gladly give you details of single and period-return fares, and of other journeys that are not shown in this leaflet.

Coaches depart DAILY THROUGHOUT THE YEAR (except Christmas Day), as follows:—

LONDON (King's Cross Coach Station) 9.00 a.m.
GLOBE ROAD (near Stepney Green Station) 9.20 a.m.
STRATFORD (Manbey Park Road, Maryland Point) 9.35 a.m.
ILFORD (Trolley Bus Standard No. 167, Roding Bridge) 9.47 a.m.
ROMFORD (17/19 Eastern Avenue) 10.02 a.m.
BRENTWOOD (The Yorkshire Grey) 10.17 a.m.
INGATESTONE (Market Place) 10.30 a.m.
CHELMSFORD (Market Road) 10.55 a.m.

Fares subject to amendment

DESTINATION	ARRIVAL TIME	RETURN TIME Mons.—Fris.	RETURN TIME Sats.	RETURN TIME Sundays	LONDON DAY RETURN FARE*
MAPLESTEAD, The Pump ...	11.45 a.m.	6.20 p.m.	3.55 p.m.	7.44 p.m.	8/9
SUDBURY, Old Market Place ...	12.00 nn.	6.05 p.m.	3.40 p.m.	7.30 p.m.	9/3
NEWTON, Bus Shelter ...	12.10 p.m.	5.45 p.m.	3.25 p.m.	7.20 p.m.	10/3
BOXFORD, The Fleece ...	12.20 p.m.	5.35 p.m.	3.15 p.m.	7.10 p.m.	10/3
HADLEIGH, Market Place ...	12.35 p.m.	5.20 p.m.	3.00 p.m.	6.55 p.m.	10/3
LONG MELFORD, Post Office ...	12.12 p.m.	5.43 p.m.	3.23 p.m.	7.22 p.m.	9/3
GLEMSFORD, Broadway ...	12.20 p.m.	5.35 p.m.	3.15 p.m.	7.10 p.m.	10/3
STANSTEAD, Bridge Corner ...	12.25 p.m.	5.30 p.m.	3.10 p.m.	7.05 p.m.	10/3
HARTEST. The Green ...	12.35 p.m.	5.20 p.m.	3.00 p.m.	6.55 p.m.	10/3
ACTON, The Crown ...	12.20 p.m.	5.45 p.m.	3.20 p.m.	7.17 p.m.	10/3
GT. WALDINGFIELD, Heards Corner ...	12.23 p.m.	5.42 p.m.	3.17 p.m.	7.14 p.m.	10/3
LT. WALDINGFIELD, Steeds Corner ...	12.26 p.m.	5.39 p.m.	3.14 p.m.	7.10 p.m.	10/3
LAVENHAM, The Swan ...	12.35 p.m.	5.30 p.m.	3.05 p.m.	7.05 p.m.	10/3
BRENT ELEIGH, Post Office ...	12.42 p.m.	5.23 p.m.	2.58 p.m.	6.59 p.m.	10/6
MONKS ELEIGH, Post Office ...	12.47 p.m.	5.18 p.m.	2.53 p.m.	6.54 p.m.	10/6
CHELSWORTH, Post Office ...	12.50 p.m.	5.15 p.m.	2.50 p.m.	6.51 p.m.	10/6
BILDESTON, Market Place ...	12.55 p.m.	5.10 p.m.	2.45 p.m.	6.48 p.m.	10/6
HITCHAM. White Horse ...	12.59 p.m.	5.06 p.m.	2.41 p.m.	6.43 p.m.	10/9
FINBOROUGH, Council Houses ...	1.11 p.m.	4.54 p.m.	2.29 p.m.	6.35 p.m.	10/9
STOWMARKET, Barnards Garage ...	1.20 p.m.	4.45 p.m.	2.20 p.m.	6.30 p.m.	10/9

*PLEASE NOTE that Day-Return Fares at lower rates are available from ROMFORD, BRENTWOOD, INGATESTONE, CHELMSFORD

CONNECTIONS may be made for CAVENDISH, CLARE and a host of other attractive villages.

The Company's services are operated subject to published Conditions of Carriage, which may be inspected at any Office of the Company.

CORONA COACHES LTD.   Head Office : Old Market Place, Sudbury, Suffolk   Phone : Sudbury 2193

then the Vega was becoming slightly dated. DGV, the 33-seater, was Warner's bus on the Hadleigh run, while one of the 29-seaters was allocated to Plumb, on Hartest. The London service was maintained by the true work-horses of the fleet, half-cab machines that looked more ancient than any of the rest – Jokey had the Regal III and Charley Gilson had one or other of the two Leylands. It says something for the traffic that the service could be maintained with a 33 and a 35 seater, but it must be remembered that the permitted box dimensions for a two-axle coach were still eight feet by 30 feet (2.4 x 9.1 metres). Only four of the 11 coaches were diesel, yet the annual mileage of those on the London service was prohibitive for petrol engined coaches – pushing 62,000 a year for Charley's vehicle and still more for Jokey's.

For our own use we had two cars - a Humber Super Snipe that Bert had bought second-hand in Birmingham and an elderly Austin Twelve-Six that we had acquired with the business. In this I commuted from Hadstock; on one icy morning I lost control on the bends east of Sturmer and only avoided a ten-foot drop into a field by managing to point the car at a telephone post. Some weeks later, when the front of the car had been straightened out, Billy Bird brought it round from the workshop with the remark: "Here it is, Guv'nor and they've moved all the telephone poles back into the fields". I think it was then I felt myself accepted.

Getting to grips

One of the first things that Bert suggested to me was that, as the Director responsible for traffic, I ought to take over the preparation of the daily duty sheet. Allocation of crews to vehicles and services had been largely a matter of tradition and Len Hazell seldom diverged from established practice. The operations were not demanding enough for the definition of formal 'duties', but we were not quite sure we wanted to keep the same man always on the same journey and the drivers were not altogether happy either. One thing we discovered was that the Ipswich service was the preserve of Bill Sandford, known as Snigley - I conducted it one Tuesday soon after we took over and learnt a lot. The licence provided for direct operation between Little Wadingfield and Monks Eleigh, but to begin with I found that Snigley had diverted the service to go round by Brent Eleigh, past his sister's bungalow, where he would stop for a cup of tea and her shopping list. We wondered whether to apply to change the licensed route, but an objection from Eastern Counties would have been certain, so we had to alter Snigley's habits instead which caused some resentment – which was outweighed by the satisfaction of passengers who had to wait in the coach while he had his tea. Then, again, we lost a couple of regular passengers from Brent Eleigh.

What fascinated me, though, was what happened when we reached Ipswich. The terminus was the "Half Moon and Star"; all the private operators used Inns as their terminal in Ipswich – and we parked in the road alongside. When everyone was off, Snigley and I went into the public bar, where I was instructed to give the landlord two shillings out of the bag - this was the fee for using the Inn as our terminal – despite the fact that we could never have got GGV into the yard at the back. Naturally we had a half-a-pint apiece and then went our separate ways (what Snigley did I never knew – I suppose it was his sister's shopping – but I had to see a printer about our timetables). At half past three we met back at the Inn and had a further pint (Ipswich pubs being open all day on market day) and then I saw what the fee was for.

At the back of the Inn was a yard, into which the horse-drawn carriers' carts would once have turned, and in the yard stood a substantial brick shed. This was now filled with all sorts of goods and parcels, which an elderly man in a brown coat was busy sorting out. There were rolls of chicken wire; linoleum; even some livestock, which fortunately was not coming with us. Each of the buses that stood outside was being loaded up, for the passengers as they did their shopping had only to say, "Send it to the 'Half Moon and Star' for the Corona" and during the afternoon this was done. It strikes me as a very sensible way of organising the retail trade in co-ordination with public transport.

As the days passed we got to know the people with whom we were to share our lives – the staff (and the booking agents), the passengers and our competitors. In this our most valuable friend turned out to be Maude Swindells, whose loyalty to the firm meant that we were accepted as soon as she saw that we were keen to do well in it. Her sense of humour and her fund of stories were well matched by her tactful way of keeping us informed as to 'what was going on' - not that we had any serious problems in the area so unhappily called 'man management'. Indeed, the firm was quite truly a sort of extended family and there were one or two of the drivers who could have run it as well as we could. (I said as much to Jokey once and he said he wouldn't want the responsibility). I can remember only a few arguments over duties and any problems over pay were settled promptly, on the facts of the matter, so that they could not rankle.

In fact and without exception, the drivers went out of their way from the first to work with us. They took particular pride in introducing us to the local pubs, with a view to securing the coach bookings for the darts clubs and the pub outings and some of our private hire customers would request that a driver of their choice took them out. We learnt about the past, too: Bill Swindells and Snigley had driven the old charabancs and in those days the Felixstowe road was noted for the police speed traps. When they had both been caught, Mr. Chinery decided to take a party there himself, only to be prosecuted – the evidence, to his everlasting disgust, being given by a constable who had timed him (at 14 mph) on a bicycle (the legal limit for a chara was 12 mph). On an empty run to London one night the acetylene tail-lamp failed and Bill spotted a long line of lanterns where the road was under repair. He told Snigley to get down on the running-board and pick one up to hang over the back, but what they did not know was that the whole line was attached to a chain. The noise sent them on their way in a hurry.

The booking agents were almost part of the business too and we were dependent upon them for the excursion bookings from the villages, as well as for much of the London traffic. Some of them had been with Corona from the early days of the London service, particularly Miss Hogg at Hadleigh, Mr. Cutting at Glemsford and Miss Redgrave at Hartest (a formidable lady – somewhat irreverently known to us as 'the Hartest Virgin'). Mr. Fisk at Lavenham and Mr. Blythe at Long Melford had their shops just where the London coaches picked up and took a proprietorial interest in the service with which they had been associated for so long and so did Mr. Hunt at Halstead. At Great Waldingfield, the timing point – Heard's Corner – was named after our agent's shop.

Bookings from London were undertaken by PSV Operators Ltd., who leased the land in the Pentonville Road on which the temporary Kings Cross Coach Station stood. The station manager became a good friend and we soon got to know many of the drivers on other companies' services whose route we shared as far as Chelmsford – Blackwell and Grey-Green in particular. The refreshment halt was at Widford, just on the London side of the town, where the down coaches stopped at the 'White Horse' and the up coaches at a cafe across the road, owned, I believe, by Snigley's father-in-law. At both places there would be free coffee and rolls for the drivers and the 'White Horse' made a small cash payment as well.

As the season built up, Bert and I spent more and more

time upon the road and we got to know many of our passengers on a personal basis. There was Mr. Eastaugh of Brent Eleigh, with whom my wife and I became friendly and there was the gentleman from the level-crossing cottage at Redbridge (whose daughter kept the gates and who turned out to be a Polish prince). Our local 'character' was Mr Tombs, who lived at Acton and went to Sudbury each Thursday to do his shopping in quite flamboyant style – a red waistcoat and yellow stockings with his knickerbockers. The Thursday afternoon market service was a perfect example of rural transport – as the bus came through the Acton street it stopped at almost every cottage and the conductor had to get down, help the old ladies out with their bags and sometimes even carry the shopping to the door, find the key under the mat and let the lady in.

Quite soon we were working for the railway. Mr. Postle, the Stationmaster, who became a good friend of ours, rang Bert one evening and asked if we could put on a bus to Haverhill and back, as there were some wagons off the line at Glemsford. Eastern National would take too long to get over from Halstead, he said and he had authority to pay us. So Bert took one of the *Tigers* and made the trip. When he got to Sudbury station a few passengers got in, followed by the Guard, with his flags and case, who immediately went to the back of the bus. This meant that when any one wanted to alight he had to walk up to the front and ring the bell and open the door – but the Guard clearly belonged in those days at the rear of his train. Even then the traffic was very thin on the Stour Valley line, yet when it came up for closure some ten years later there was an outcry and I myself came in for personal abuse in the local paper.

It was a fascinating world and one into which we soon lost ourselves. At first we held board meetings, with our wives present (they were Directors, for obvious tax reasons), but Eric Osborne could seldom join us and we did not keep the practice up long. One reason was that we were already running into trouble and I know Bert did not want to admit it. The hard fact was that the London service had been neglected and the company's income was not what we had allowed for. That first spring we had what today would be called a 'cash flow' problem and I guaranteed an overdraft of £500 – a quarter of the value of my house. This turned our minds to new developments

RIGHT: CCF 120, new to Long in 1949 stands at Kings Cross. *(Author's collection)*

and Bert came into the office at Sudbury one day with the suggestion, gained from talking to passengers and staff, that we should recast the London timetable.

First, though, we had to increase our fares. We were members of No. 6 Regional Fares Committee and, against our better judgement, we had to go along with their applications to add twelve-and-a-half per cent to summer weekend fares on the London service. I could see the logic of this where there was strong holiday traffic, but I felt we had a different market,

which it would not be wise to soak in this way. The compromise was that the increase would only be applied to stages where we were competing with Eastern National and Eastern Counties. The Metropolitan Traffic Commissioner would not allow us to be 'different'.

Then we saw the possibility of a bit of new local traffic, all because a group of schoolgirls used to catch the 5 pm from Sudbury to Lavenham (the down London coach) rather than hang about for the train, despite the fact they had BR season

31

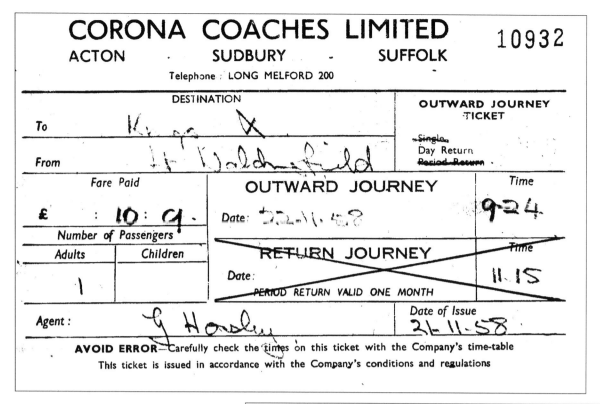

CORONA COACHES LIMITED   10932

ACTON · SUDBURY - SUFFOLK

Telephone : LONG MELFORD 200

DESTINATION	OUTWARD JOURNEY TICKET
To *K...* X	~~Single~~
From *Gt Waldingfield*	Day Return ~~Period Return~~

Fare Paid	OUTWARD JOURNEY	Time
£ : 10 : 9 .	Date: *22-11-58*	9·24
Number of Passengers	~~RETURN JOURNEY~~	~~Time~~
Adults	Children	Date:	11·15
1		PERIOD RETURN VALID ONE MONTH	
Agent : *G Horsley*		Date of Issue *21-11-58*

AVOID ERROR—Carefully check the times on this ticket with the Company's time-table

This ticket is issued in accordance with the Company's conditions and regulations

---

tickets paid for by the County Council. With what proved good traffic sense we put on a bus at 8.20 am from Lavenham to Sudbury, with return journeys at 6 pm Mondays to Fridays and 12.45 pm on Saturdays. This was the first time that Lavenham, Acton and Great Waldingfield people could get a bus to Sudbury for work and later on it required a double-decker in the mornings. At the same time we tidied up the local Acton–Sudbury service, deleting some Saturday evening journeys, dating from the time before farm workers got a Saturday half day, but which had not in fact run for a good many years. We also scheduled some empty running, where the morning feeder coaches went from Sudbury to Acton and back to refuel. These revisions went into effect on 23 April 1956 and at the same time we moved the Sudbury terminal for our local services from Market Hill to our own premises at Old Market Place.

Traffic began to look up with the better weather and before long we were experiencing our first Easter peak. I had been given a notebook in which Mr. Chinery had recorded the loadings for each weekend for the post-war years and this formed the basis of our planning. The Easter weekend was the busiest of the year, with traffic building up from the Thursday until most people returned home on the Monday afternoon and evening. The heavier flow went back to London, but the down journeys always needed relieving too and the total requirement could be as many as 20 coaches, of the size then available. Most of these had to be hired, of course, although at the time we had no local services to run on the Bank Holiday and limited ourselves to one coach on a Clacton excursion; but the problem was the interval that followed from Easter to Whitsun, when demand fell right back, yet this was when the bills for vehicle hire came in.

Many of our neighbours – and competitors – were regular collaborators in this way and I had learned when with Premier Travel how useful this could be; Beeston

CORONA COACHES LTD.,

SUDBURY,

SUFFOLK.

EXPRESS SERVICES ONLY

E 9600

OUTWARD JOURNEY	PERIOD	DAY	SINGLE
FOR CONDITIONS SEE NOTICES	SERVICE No. *1A*		

FROM *Boxford*	DAY *Sunday*
PICK UP AT	DATE *23-11-58*
Fleece	A.M.	P.M. *7-10*

TO *Chelmsford*	DAY
PICK UP ON RETURN AT	DATE
	A.M.	P.M.

PASSENGERS	FARE	TOTAL
ADULTS *Two*	4/9	9	6
CHILDREN			
ISSUED BY *Liddleston*	DATE OF ISSUE *22 11 58*	TOTAL FARE £	9	6

IF IT'S TRAVEL CORONA WILL HELP YOU

CORONA COACHES LTD.

OLD MARKET PLACE,
SUDBURY,
SUFFOLK.

SUDBURY 2193

ACTON,
SUDBURY,
SUFFOLK.

TIME TABLES

OF

LOCAL BUS SERVICES

FROM 17th JUNE 1957 UNTIL FURTHER NOTICE

FOR DETAILS OF CORONA EXPRESS SERVICES TO AND FROM LONDON, STOWMARKET, HADLEIGH AND HARTEST, SEE EXPRESS SERVICE TIMETABLES

The Services shown in this Leaflet are operated subject to the Company's standard conditions of carriage which may be inspected at any office of the Company.

BANK HOLIDAY ARRANGEMENTS

ALL SERVICES ARE SUBJECT TO ALTERATION DURING BANK HOLIDAY PERIODS. PASSENGERS SHOULD ENQUIRE FOR DETAILS. NO SERVICES WILL OPERATE ON CHRISTMAS DAY.

Price 1d.

S.6/57/40

33

and Rule would put the same drivers on whenever they worked for us and those men knew the Hadleigh road or the one from Lavenham as well as ours did. Other subcontractors were Long, on the Hartest road and Taylor of Bildeston. It was useful revenue for them, continuing to a smaller extent on Sundays throughout the summer and again at Christmas. We never hired from Theobald of Long Melford, our nearest neighbour; his vehicles were hardly suitable, it is true, but the reason had more to do with local rivalry, which also accounts for the rarity of our hiring from Chambers of Bures, who did have better coaches available. The problem was that one never knew the likely loadings back to London until Charlie Gilson, the outstation driver, rang from Kings Cross at 9 am on the Monday to report the day-return bookings, which could depend a lot upon the weather. Mr. Beeston used to keep a coach free for us which he would turn out and drive at short notice if we needed it.

The local firms varied in their attitude to us. The Beestons became very friendly and impressed us with the high standard of their fleet of small, light brown coaches. Mr. Taylor and his two sons struck me as surly and suspicious, though always reliable; old 'Tummy' Theobald kept his distance. Newton Rule was reserved, too, as were the Chambers brothers; Corona shared the Sudbury private hire work with Chambers, Rule and Theobald, so we were close competitors in an unregulated market. Only with Eddie Long did I feel anything warmer, which was to stand me in good stead later on, starting from the day when I sat in his traffic office at Glemsford, negotiating the re-timing of the London services. Long had objected, but I did not want to divert the Traffic Court case away from the main issues, where I would have to fight the combine companies and the railway, so I offered a limitation on certain journeys, to protect his local bus services. Eddie looked at me and said, "I do believe you're an honest man, Mr. Hibbs" – which says something about the general state of affairs. (Another discovery was a draft for the merger of Long's and Chinery's businesses, proposed just before the war, which had come to nothing).

Changing the London times

This was to be a major change, but we had no doubt that something had to be done. The majority of our passengers, supported by our drivers, held that it had been a great mistake not to reinstate the pre-war timetable, with its good day-return facility to London. The extra timings on Fridays and summer Wednesdays were an awkward compromise and expensive to operate. These now disappeared – we contemplated making the up journey at 7.30 am daily, but this was ruled out by drivers' hours regulations. The up afternoon journey was delayed on Mondays to Fridays, giving longer time for shopping in Stowmarket as well as an improved day-return facility out of London. The weekend timings we altered less, except for bringing the 4.30 pm out of London back to 2 pm, so as to add a later journey back from Stowmarket. This was much appreciated by our weekend passengers, who could now leave later and it also relieved the need to duplicate the earlier timing. On the other hand, the up journey on Saturday afternoons required a relief at least as far as Chelmsford throughout the year and usually through to Kings Cross, so we scheduled it back at 11.15 pm, offering a chance for people to get to the theatre in London. This loaded well enough to justify its existence, scheduling light running at little extra labour cost, and it was not as unpopular with the drivers as might have been thought – later on it would pass my house in the Melford Road in the small hours, with usually a finger on the horn button as the coach went by.

When we had got all this arranged we realised that we would be removing some local facilities that were moderately well used and where there could be a comparable loss of traffic for the London journeys with the removal of the day return facility. We also thought that we might be breaking faith with our regular customers. So, rather as an afterthought, for we were working under pressure to get the London timings revised, we decided to retain the afternoon journeys, Mondays to Fridays, from Bildeston to Halstead, back to Stowmarket and finally back to Acton, with a Sunday evening journey from Sudbury to Stowmarket as well. The weekday journeys only loaded at all well on Thursdays (market day at both Sudbury and Stowmarket), with the rest becoming a drain on our revenue. The drivers who usually worked them with one of the 29-seaters 'D/C' (driver conduct – what today would be OMO, or even OPO), christened the afternoon runs 'the doddle'. We also decided to end the practice of outstationing a vehicle at Barnards' premises at Stowmarket, though because Ratcliffe,

TABLE EIGHT – The London service, 1956-1959 Omitting minor timing points				
	D am	SO pm	SuO pm	MF pm	SuO pm
STOWMARKET dep	8 30	2 20	3 30	4 45	6 30
Bildeston	8 55	2 45	3 55	5 10	6 48
Lavenham	9 15	3 05	4 15	5 30	7 05
Acton	9 30	3 20	4 30	5 45	7 17
Long Melford	9 38	3 28	4 38	5 X 53	7 10
HARTEST dep	9 15	3 00	4 15	5 20	6 55
Glemsford	9 30	3 15	4 30	5 X 35	7 10
HADLEIGH dep	9 15	3 00	4 15	5 #20	6 #55
SUDBURY Old Market Place	9 50	3 40	4 50	6 05	7 30
Halstead	10 15	4 05	5 15	6 *30	7 ^50
Braintree, Bus Park	10 35	4 25	5 35	6 *50	8 ^10
Chelmsford, War Memorial	10 55	4 45	5 55	7 10	8 30
Romford, opposite Town Hall	11 48	5 38	6 48	8 03	9 23
LONDON Kings Cross Coach Station arr	12 50 1025	6 40	7 40	9 05	

	D a m	SSuO pm	MF pm	SuO pm	SO pm
LONDON Kings Cross Coach Station dep	9 00	2 00	6 00	8 15	11 15
Romford, 17-19 Eastern Avenue	10 02	3 02	6 52	9 05	11 53
Chelmsford, Market Road	10 55	3 55	7 45	9 55	1238am
Braintree, Bus Park	11 15	4~15	8*05	10@15	1 05am
Halstead	11 35	4~35	8*25	10@35	1 23am
SUDBURY Old Market Place	12 00	5 00	8 50	10 55	1 40am
HADLEIGH arr	12 35	5 35	9#25	11 30	——
Glemsford	12 20	5 X 20	9 10	11 13	——
HARTEST arr	12 35	5 35	9 25	11 28	——
Long Melford	12 12	5 X 12	9 02	11 03	1 48am
Acton	12 20	5 20	9 10	11 08	1 54am
Lavenham	12 35	5 25	9 25	11 20	2 08am
Bildeston	12 55	5 55	9 45	11 37	2 25am
STOWMAKET arr	1 20	6 20	10 10	11 55	——

Notes D - Daily MF - Mondays to Fridays SO - Saturdays only SSuO - Saturdays and Sundays only SuO - Sundays only - X: On these journeys passengers will not be picked up and set down between Sudbury and Glemsford; #: On these journeys passengers will not be both picked up and set down between Sudbury and Hadleigh; *: Passengers will not be conveyed between Halstead or Braintree and London or vice versa; ^: Ditto, 1 June-30 September; ~: Ditto, on Sundays; @: Ditto, 1 October-31 May.

the conductor, lived in the town, we had to license the positioning mileage as express, with the statutory minimum fare of one shilling (5p). Even so, drivers' hours regulations meant that we had to take Jokey off at Acton at 9.10 pm, which left us with an awkward shift for his replacement. In practice, Bert often covered if he hadn't been driving during the day and it left Stowmarket late enough to build up a small demand from the cinemas and the pubs.

But to plan all this was but the start of the problem, for the applications to vary the licences met with the expected objections. After meeting those of the local bus firms, such as Long, we were left with the usual expense and hassle of a major hearing at the Cambridge Traffic Court, where we were opposed by British Rail, Eastern Counties, Eastern National and Blackwell of Earls Colne. Eastern Counties only came through Sudbury in the summer, so the issue really turned upon the London traffic at Halstead and Braintree, where both Eastern National and Blackwell had claims to be the established operators. We submitted that we were only returning to the pre-war timings, but the Commissioners would not accept this in the face of the objections. Seeking a compromise, they ruled out the Eastern Counties claim for protection at Sudbury (much to our relief), but imposed restrictions on our 'new' timings at Halstead and Braintree (see Table 8). They also restricted some of our Hadleigh journeys so as to protect the slow and unpopular Eastern Counties local buses.

The whole procedure took a great deal of time and effort, culminating at a public hearing, to which we had to take the usual collection of 'witnesses'. Once we had made our case for the revisions, though, the Halstead and Braintree restrictions were imposed without reference to demand; merely to placate the objectors and to avoid an appeal. The whole thing was a ritual and a hurdle to be jumped and it seemed to me very doubtful whether the net effect of licensing was to benefit anyone at all. It did however mean that it was only on 30 July that we were able to introduce the improved timetable, by which time various other things had happened.

New routes in Essex

The local bus service that Mr. Chinery had tried to run between Sudbury and Halstead, known to the drivers as 'the dishy bus' (additional), had been a problem for some years. It seemed to us that the best way to build it up would be to take in some of the villages to the east of the main road, so we applied to divert two journeys by way of Pebmarsh (rapidly christened 'Pebblemarsh' by the drivers, who hated the dog-leg corner on the way). Since Eastern National already linked the village with Halstead we had to accept some limitations, but we were able to offer a shopping facility and a 'picture bus' to Sudbury. The diversion built up enough extra demand to make a difference, but the service was never a money-spinner. Halstead was at that time in decline and there were simply too few chimneys along the main road.

Some light relief came with a notice of grant from the Traffic Commissioners' office, in which it was observed that the timetable was now slightly too fast for the permitted maximum speed (then 30 mph). It had therefore been re-timed to comply with the law and a revised schedule was attached – showing each journey now reaching Halstead shortly after it was due to leave again. Having put this right, we were able to introduce the improved service on 2 June.

In the meantime we had been faced with a new challenge. Harry Rippingale had been running a little group of bus services from the village of Gestingthorpe from a very early date and at this time possessed a fleet of four Bedfords (see Appendix 3), two of which had been new in 1948 and 1949, when traffic was

booming. 'Bluffy' was a well-known character, regularly to be seen at the wheel of his bus on Sudbury Market Hill; he would sit inside as the passengers got off, collecting their fares in a pudding basin. "Thankye me old dear", he would say, "See yer when yer come hoom, me old dear", in the very local dialect. Despite this cavalier attitude to charging, Bluffy had a set of tickets which were kept on the rack for issue when word reached him (as it always seemed to) that there were Traffic Examiners around; tickets that were carefully recovered from passengers when they had no further use for them. Similarly he always complied with the law by carrying a printed timetable (of which he told me that there were six copies in existence; this document, incidentally, bore no relationship to either his licensed or his actual operations).

We had been running the business for little more than a month when word came by way of one of our drivers that Mr. Rippingale would like to see us with a view to selling his business. His routes linked the villages of Gestingthorpe, Belchamp Walter (known locally as Walter Belchamp) and Wickham St. Paul with Sudbury, Halstead and Braintree, taking in a number of places on the way and fitting in to a complex share-out with the services of Jennings, Amos, Letch and Pyman. We consulted the drivers and learned that there had been previous negotiations with Eastern National which had fallen through. When Bert and I talked to Mr. & Mrs. Rippingale in the dark living room at Gestingthorpe we were warned obliquely that they had decided to sell and would rather we had the business than Eastern National, but if we didn't buy it, then . . . .

As we drove back to Acton we made acid comments about blackmail but it was plain that we had a problem. If Eastern National bought the business we could forget any hope of developments south and west of Sudbury. I had taken a copy of the timetables and I satisfied myself as to the actual car workings (which made it plain that passengers were being carried on several ostensibly empty journeys), while Bert had looked over the fleet. A few days later we arrived at a plan.

We had been developing local bus services on a rather larger scale than the Chinery management had allowed for and I could immediately see where many of the Rippingale timings could be fitted in with our own. I went over to Cambridge and obtained several sheets of timing graph paper from Premier Travel and then sat down to produce my own set of car workings, with an eye to the revisions we were already planning and some modification of the Rippingale timings here and there. The results looked promising and I told Bert I could run the services as they existed with only two of Bluffy's vehicles and then improve on that by careful re-timing. Bert spoke to Eric, who put us in touch with Bakers of Aldershot and we got some figures for the sale prices we might expect. Then we had a board meeting and with Eric's agreement decided to go ahead. To find the money we sold the two newest Rippingale vehicles, a bus and a coach, on the day we took over and persuaded Bluffy to leave £1000 for payment in the following year. This gave us a 29-seater and a 20-seater, neither of them in the best of condition, which we quickly had painted in Corona chocolate and tangerine. We also took on one driver, but he was never popular with our own men and he did not stay long

He was however of vital importance in the early days, while we were learning the routes – most of the licences just said 'via unclassified roads' and the timetable was not much help either. There was one lane – Chapel Hill, near Belchamp Walter – which we covered once a week and on the first Thursday I conducted with the new driver. As we came to a cottage he told me to look out for a shopping bag hanging on the gate; if it was not there the two old ladies would not be coming today. (I wonder still whether Eastern National could have been able to pass that information on, as I did to our other drivers). They were certainly there that day along with many others, come to try out the new firm. On the Saturday afternoon we ran a 37 and a 38-seater into Sudbury, where Bluffy would have had a 29 and a 20. I conducted GGV, the 38-seater and as the 50th passenger got on at Bulmer Tye he remarked to me how nice it was to have a bit of room. (On Market Hill I opened the rear emergency door and got a few of them out that way, with an eye on the constable across the road). The Thursday circular service round the back lanes at Bulmer had been acquired from Pat Brown, so a second of his routes had joined Corona – it seemed to exist chiefly for two large families living in Smeetham Hall Lane.

As might be expected, the crowds were reduced in subsequent weeks. We found ourselves running through Borley and jokes were made about not even the ghost turning up. But the local Vicar presented us with a petition carrying many signatures, asking for the afternoon journey to be diverted by way of the Green; we put it on, but after the first week it did well to find more than two passengers there. Neither did we succeed in keeping much of Bluffy's private hire work; in my experience you seldom do after a takeover. People find it convenient to make a change they have often considered and goodwill in this sense is money down the drain.

A settling-in period

Already it will be plain that my first months of management were fully occupied. The Ipswich service was another problem and perhaps took more of my time than its once a week operation could justify. The direct route from Sudbury was the preserve of Eastern Counties, whose timetables had not been altered since the days of solid tyres. As a result their buses had to wait at Hadleigh to make up time, so that the service was more a barrier than a connection between Sudbury and Ipswich. Even though our services went round 'half West Suffolk' its running time was three minutes less than Eastern Counties and some people preferred it. I drove round the area looking for ways to improve the service, even at the expense of Snigley's sister's shopping and discovered one village in Eastern Counties territory that had no bus to Ipswich at all. So the revised route diverted 'via unclassified' to serve Lindsey Tye and we converted the licence to stage carriage so as to offer intermediate fares and fares to and from Hadleigh. All this was introduced on 3 July.

Earlier on, though, we had to deal with the problems of tickets and cash control. There was a fairly standard system of duplicate vouchers for bookings on the London services, and excursions and of course we had to accept the PSV Operators vouchers from their agents throughout London. One oddity was the practice of accepting bookings by post, which we looked at with suspicion. An example of the pre-printed postcard is shown on Page 31 and we saw at once how it could lend itself to misuse. The Kings Cross people disliked it too, because it reduced their commission. All the same, quite a lot of regular passengers used it, many of whom did not have a booking office near their homes - indeed, as will be seen, the system gave us a valuable idea of the extent of our catchment area; far wider than just Greater London. So we compromised and arranged for tickets booked in this way to be sent out with the conductor's waybill, so that they could only be handed over in exchange for cash.

I doubt whether there had been any actual misuse, because our passengers and staff alike were extremely honest, which was one of the reasons why the business was such a pleasure to run. As we have seen, the conductor left the coach at Braintree or Chelmsford so as to return by the down working, which meant there could be no secure check on over-riding on the up journeys. We wondered whether we ought to appoint an inspector, but turned it down; for one thing it would have undermined the relationship of trust – Charley Gilson and Jokey felt it was as much their service as ours; and in any case it would have cost a good deal more than we might hope to save. As it was, Bert and I were always working alongside the staff, so we knew pretty well what was going on.

At busy times I would go up on one of the relief coaches and load the vehicles away from Kings Cross, working my way down from one to another so as to collect most of the voucher tickets before the conductor came on – he could hardly have cleared the whole convoy between Braintree and Sudbury. In that way I got to know the problems, too, like finding your passengers at Manbey Park Road, Stratford, on a Bank Holiday Friday evening, with ten of our coaches (some hired), two or three of Blackwells and innumerable vehicles belonging to Grey Green or Suttons of Clacton. With our coaches working through to the feeder routes it could be no mean achievement to get everyone on the right vehicle so that no-one had to change at Sudbury.

At busy times it was often necessary to relieve the morning departure from 'the Cross', which was done as often as possible by laying over a relief that had worked up with Charley Gilson the previous evening. This meant a lodging payment for the driver and several of the men used a small hotel not far from the coach station. Some, though, preferred to take the lodging payment and sleep on the back seat and we decided that this was something that ought to be discouraged. So at Bert's suggestion and with Billy Bird's approval as Shop Steward we replaced the cash payment with an arrangement with the hotel whereby drivers who spent the night there brought the bill home and we settled it through the post. Sleeping on the back seat was banned. Some years later the writer George Ewart Evans told me about a medieval Abbot in East Anglia who had the same problem when he sent his carter to the market at Ipswich; he took the money and slept under his cart. I did not discover whether the Abbot found the same answer to his problem.

For local traffic, including the country end of the London service, we inherited a ticket system called 'Bellgraphic' (see Appendix 4). Inside a large flat metal box there would be a pack of tickets folded concertinawise, with a duplicate set interleaved throughout. When properly inserted the top ticket showed in a square opening on the top of a sort of canister, while its duplicate slipped under a carbon sheet beneath it. To issue a ticket you wrote the fare in pencil on the top copy (there were spaces for single and return) and worked a lever at the side. That slid the top copy out, to be torn off and given to the passenger, while the duplicate remained in the canister.

The system was simple and foolproof (though the art of loading the canister had to be practised and was a problem if you ran out in the middle of a busy trip). But the machines were getting old and there was an unnecessary burden in the office work that was involved. One of Maude Swindells' daily tasks was to sort out the duplicate tickets from their packs, total up the cash and in effect complete the waybill (all the conductor had to do was to enter the starting number for each journey). Any further analysis to allocate data to services, where waybills covered more than one route, had to wait until that preliminary work had been done, while, worst of all, the driver or conductor did not know whether his takings had been right until the waybill had been made up in the office, no sooner than the day after he had paid in.

This was a system we did not like. When I worked as a conductor with Premier Travel I had used the Setright 'Insert' system, where a card ticket was inserted into a machine which then printed the appropriate details on it when a handle was turned. This, as with the Bellgraphic, had the great advantage over the old Bell Punch of doing away with the need for tickets that carried a pre-printed value, with consequent problems of audit. The alternative was the Setright 'Speed', which printed from a blank roll inside the machine, avoiding the need for a ticket rack, but heavier to carry.

We borrowed a machine of each kind from the manufacturers and tried them out. I explained to Billy Bird, as Shop Steward, that the purpose of changing to Setright was, on the one hand, to be fairer to the staff, who would now pay in on the machine reading at the end of each duty and, on the other, to transfer much of Maude's work to the road staff, who would have to enter more information on their waybills and add it up themselves. He agreed that it was sensible, as drivers and conductors on rural services have a fair amount of spare time and he reported that the staff on the whole preferred the 'Insert' machines.

So we ordered seven, some bought outright and some rented and designed the ticket system to go with them. (See Appendix 4). This was quite complicated, including an 'exchange' ticket to be issued against vouchers collected on the London service, so that all passenger journeys were recorded on the waybill instead of having to add some in the office. A lot of people used the London service without pre-booking and while we always stated publicly that pre-booking was necessary, we could not afford to turn them away. So there were special tickets for the London service and since the range of the machines was limited we had to have a special day return ticket worth ten shillings more than the value printed. Ticket and fare enthusiasts will be interested in Appendix 4, which is a set of instructions for the use of the Setrights. I designed the waybill and later modified it to include allocated (not average) costs against each journey, so as to arrive at net revenue. This work would have been done in the office, but I wonder whether it is done anywhere today, using a computer programme.

Thanks to everyone's good will, the system was a success and worked smoothly from the start. Our two conductresses (part-time), the wives of Billy Bird and Gordon Clampin, took to it, which was important. On weekdays the 5 pm from Sudbury ('the doddle') could be busy as far as Acton but very quiet thereafter, so it was possible for one of the girls to conduct that far and then hand bag and punch to her husband and go home to get the tea. Otherwise they worked full duties on Thursdays and Saturdays and, as well as the money, they enjoyed the work and had a chance to do their shopping as well. If their husbands were not available I would team them up with Bert or one of the older men.

For my own part I conducted a duty each Thursday and a double shift on Saturdays, as soon as the additional stage mileage began to produce set duties of the traditional kind. I was still living at Hadstock and driving 35 miles each way over what were very indifferent roads – on Saturdays I used to leave the car at Gestingthorpe and conduct the 9.15 am into Sudbury, picking it up again after leaving the 10.15 pm. Bert did his share of the driving, chiefly on the local services but also on London at the weekends and sometimes he would take a coastal excursion when he might be able to take Ena and the girls with him if there was room. The private hire work and the specialist tours that we developed we left firmly to the full-time staff, for whom the tips were important (I found I got a rough idea of who made the most 'dropsy' and that told me which of the drivers the public liked best). At Bert's suggestion we moved our office down to Sudbury, though he continued to spend more of his time at Acton, supervising the running sheds and the workshop.

As our first season came to an end I had more time to work on the revisions to the Rippingale services and to rationalise our local operations. I found great satisfaction spending the evenings with a drawing board on my knee, ruler and pencil to hand, creating new car workings, crew duties and timetables. This was a childhood dream come true. You have to get the most out of your fleet while at the same time producing fair shifts for the staff and still run the buses at the times people want them (I have seen too many schedules that sacrifice the third for the sake of the first two of these objectives). One pair of Saturday duties I tailored to my own requirements so that they brought me into Sudbury for long enough intervals to keep an eye on things and type out the duty sheet for Sunday. (This went up to Acton on the 5 pm to be posted up in the old running shed). I enjoyed conducting, though and found myself dropping into the local dialect - I suppose it made it easier to understand what was being said.

I soon discovered the local names for many places on our routes; names not to be found on the maps. I followed a practice I learned from Erskine MacPherson at Premier, putting these in to the published timetable. I like to think that in this way I was able to preserve names like the Four Releet at Milden and Seven Sisters at Gestingthorpe. The foundry at Gestingthorpe was long since gone, but Foundry Corner remained, for the information of archaeologists. Others were already records – Steeds Corner at Little Waldingfield took its name form the mansion there which we were told was owned by the brother of Wickham Steed, the former editor of *The Times*. Seven Forms, on the other hand, a timing point on one of Rippingale's routes, was a puzzle to me, until I asked our Polish prince about it and he told me that a 'form' meant a barrow, although the absence of the word tumulus on the map must have meant that those barrows had been long ploughed over.

I learned some new dialect words, too. The combine harvesters in those days were a byword for leaking seed so that when the crop was ready there would be wild oats all over the field, which had to be pulled out by hand before cutting could start. This made room for casual labour and one day the two conductresses were not available, because they were 'oating' (pronounced "oot'n", with emphasis on the first syllable and with a short vowel-sound). Then there was a word now I think lost; 'hinder', as an acronym for yonder. Maude remembered hearing it said of a pair of wood pigeons – "yonder goo the cockbird, hinder come the dow"; I liked the rhythm of that, too. And we all liked Snigley's way of saying emergency, accented on the first and third syllables.

The Rippingale revisions came in on 12 November 1956 and we published them in our first comprehensive local service timetable. The only major innovations were a Saturday service on the Braintree route and a weekday commuter facility from Halstead to Sudbury via Pebmarsh, made possible because we inherited a contract to take workmen from Sudbury to the Whitlock factory (now long gone) at Great Yeldham. Bluffy had interworked this with a school contract, but we lost both his school runs (to Halstead and Earls Colne) at the end of the first summer, so the Whitlocks bus ran light to Halstead and came home in service from there. We also found out that Whitlocks had been charging part of the cost to their staff, which meant that the service needed a licence (Bluffy had chosen not to know). They asked us at the same time to put on another contract from Long Melford, which we ran from Acton and this we were also able to licence, despite an objection form Long.

The staff position changed slightly. One or two drivers did not take to the increased amount of D/C (driver-conduct) work, as well as a rather less leisurely pace. But we were never short of staff, for there were always men who wanted to come and work for us, either full or part time and they let this be known through our own people. Among the part-timers were young 'Tutty' Eaves and that memorable character Tom Skinner, son of the Boxford operator mentioned in Chapter Two. Tom had never forgiven his father for selling the buses and despite being a successful farmer he would come and drive for us whenever he could find time, including a week of his holiday. He never wanted anything better than to cover a local duty, D/C, leaving the coach hire and excursion jobs to the full-time men.

We had inherited a fitter, but Bert was not entirely sorry when he decided to leave, whereupon Billy Bird and Bill Swindells arranged for us to meet a trained diesel mechanic who was working in one of the Sudbury factories and wanted a change. So we gained the skill and indeed the friendship of Gerald 'Bunkie' Chisnell, who stayed with us to the end and was utterly reliable. Before the war he has been a notable local soccer star who in one season scored 80 goals for Sudbury Town, with his hat-tricks going into double figures. We were unusual in the number of diesel coaches we owned (made necessary because of the high annual mileage on the London service) and Bunkie took charge of them, working with Bert in a friendly partnership. We never stood men off in the winter and several of them took turns as fitters under Bunkie's direction.

We consciously aimed to make our operations professionally sound. There had been no display of timetables anywhere, so we went to a second-hand furniture shop in Cambridge and bought some picture frames. Bert fitted them with metal backplates and we went round getting permission to put them up as soon as our new printed timetables had arrived. We also diverted the London service in Sudbury so that the coaches on the up journeys stopped outside the office instead of across the road. I am sure we were right to feel that things like this helped to establish the style of management we wanted (even though that one meant the coaches coming down North Street twice). With the help of some of the drivers we altered the layout of the front office, to give more room for the public and established ourselves with proper desks in the room at the back. (One summer day I was working there with the window open when the following memorable fragment of conversation floated in from East Street: "Ker-rist, I wouldn't want ter fall in love with the likes of 'ee")

When I had produced the set duties Bert made duty boards and the production of daily orders became simpler We never developed a rota because of the need to keep a flexible system to provide for a fair share out of the excursion and private hire work, including the need to get the right man for the right job; some customers specified a particular driver and not everyone was suited to the new excursions we were introducing, like Windsor and the Norfolk Tour, which included a leisurely drive and two stopping places to visit. Its success led me to put on a Suffolk Tour on the same lines, giving time in both Southwold and Aldeburgh, though I finished up with egg on my face. On the way home the route was by way of Needham Market, but I had not checked the detail and on the first trip Billy Bird, who was driving, found himself up against a really low railway bridge and had to reverse into a builders' yard and find another way round.

The public liked the new tours, though and we put on new ones each season. They made a better margin than Clacton at 4s9d (24p). We found that the coastal excursions were making a net loss during the school holidays, so we used a condition of the licence to increase the child's fare from half to two-thirds of the adult price. On the other hand, evening tours at 2s6d (twelve and a half pence) could be very worth while if they could be worked into a man's guaranteed day, as was usually possible on a Sunday. There were three of them on the licence, but I soon discovered that the specified routes meant nothing. Each driver had his own chosen pub and the tours offered two hours driving round the lanes and an hour's drinking time, with a suitable appreciation by the landlord of the wisdom of the driver's choice. We ran them throughout the season, on Sunday afternoons and evenings, and on Wednesdays (early closing day) the afternoon tours stopped at a suitable teashop.

Few of the new destinations were included on our destination blinds, so Bert made a set of boards with spring clips (made of clock springs) to hold them to the front windscreens. We also made a rule that 'RELIEF' should never be shown – if a down London coach was scheduled to turn short at Lavenham it was to show Lavenham. I think we both felt a great deal of satisfaction at dealing with things like this.

As the year ended, though and the weather worsened, traffic fell off and news came of pay negotiations. We benefited by Bert's decision that we should tell the men that we were prepared to match any national settlement, but our costs were staring to rise as our revenue fell. The Rippingale routes were beginning to make a better return, though and we hoped for a better season in 1957. We were working hard and we seemed to be paying our way, but we could not foresee what was about to come upon us: Suez.

RIGHT: The Bedford/Duple 'Super Vega', GGV 823, waits to bring tour passengers back from Woburn Abbey. *(P. J. Snell)*

Chapter Five

DIFFICULT TIMES

Of course, we ought to have foreseen things sooner. The Israeli attack on Egypt began on 29 October 1956 and on 6 November the first British troops landed (after what had seemed to me an interminable delay since the official ultimatum), while at the same time there was a disastrous run on the pound. I remember the feeling of shock, not just because it all seemed wrong, but because the British could not even do the wrong thing efficiently. At first the drivers were very much against it, the more left-wing men seeing it as a capitalist war and wanting no part in it, but as time passed I noticed a subtle change and a growing jingoism. I was the more bitter because of the way we were handing the Hungarian people over to Soviet Russia and I was envious of the way Premier Travel were able to send a coach (driven by my old friend Harry Law) to the Austrian border with toys and goods. Harry came back with refugees, but Mrs. Lainson, who had gone with him, stayed to do welfare work.

What was taking our attention was a licensing battle. On 17 September I had opened *Notices & Proceedings*, the publication in which applications were listed, to find that 'the companies comprising Associated Motorways' were asking for a licence for a daily express service between Cheltenham and Felixstowe. (Associated Motorways was a group of big companies in South Wales, the Midlands and the South West who operated coach services 'in pool', with a connecting hub at Cheltenham coach station; forerunners to National Express). When Bert came in from Acton I showed him the application and he asked what it had got to do with us. I told him what I thought and he agreed.

The proposed service crossed our own at Braintree. I did some work on our postal bookings and confirmed my suspicion that we had a lot of passengers from the West Country. The danger was that booking agents for Associated Motorways would channel traffic from a very wide area on to the new service and that the passengers would be met at Braintree by people with cars, with whom they were going to stay. I had no doubt that the new service would be a great benefit to the public, but I was equally certain that we ought to use the licensing machinery to protect our profits.

We objected, as did Premier Travel, Grey Green and one or two others. (Not, be it noted, the Railway Executive or Eastern Counties – most of the Associated Motorways companies were also part of the British Transport Commission). Since the primary application was in the Western Traffic Area we had to go to Bristol for a two-day hearing and then to Oxford, where the 'backing' applications for the Eastern, East Midland and Metropolitan Traffic Areas were considered at a joint sitting. Just to confuse things the Western commissioners granted the primary application before the Oxford hearing, but none the less, the backings were granted in an emasculated form, due to the weak evidence produced for the intermediate places served. There followed a complicated set of appeals, which took us to Oxford again for the inspector's hearing. A total of five days had been taken up, with highly paid counsel for the applicants (we took our own case) and much application of expensive management time, to say nothing of the expenses of witnesses, but, in the end, Associated Motorways were so miffed by the restrictions on the backings that they returned the primary licence.

All this was taking our attention and no doubt accounts for our unpreparedness for the consequences of Suez. On 20 November the government announced that from 17 December petrol would be rationed, but if we thought that we might benefit we ignored the fact that, at 200 miles a month, the ration was more generous than at any time during or after the war. It just made extra work in the office. The really bad news came on 4 December, when the fuel tax was raised from 2s6d (12.5p) to 3s6d (17.5p) a gallon. The petrol companies increased their price as well and petrol at the pump went up from five shillings & sixpence halfpenny (27.5p) to 6/5d (35p) a gallon, with diesel in proportion. We were paying commercial rates, of course, but our costs went straight up too.

CORONA COACHES LIMITED

Old Market Place, Sudbury, Suffolk.   Telephone : Sudbury 2193

IN CONSEQUENCE OF THE RATIONING OF FUEL, the following amendments to the Company's Services will apply on and from **MONDAY, 28th JANUARY, 1957** and until further notice.

SERVICE 1. Stowmarket–Bildeston–Lavenham–Sudbury–Halstead–London.
The 11.15 p.m. journey from London on Saturdays will be suspended until Saturday, 8th June, except that it will operate on Easter Saturday, 20th April.
The 7.21 a.m. journey from Lavenham to Stowmarket on Weekdays will commence instead at Monks Eleigh (Post Office) at 7.31 a.m.
The 10.15 p.m. journey from Stowmarket on Mondays to Fridays, and the 6.30 p.m. on Saturdays, will terminate at Monks Eleigh.

SERVICE 1B. Hartest–Sudbury–Halstead–London.
The 12.0 noon journey from Sudbury to Hartest, and the 5.20 p.m. from Hartest, on Mondays to Fridays, will be suspended.

SERVICE 11. Stowmarket–Bildeston–Lavenham–Sudbury–Halstead.
The 2.45 p.m. journey from Bildeston to Sudbury on Mondays to Fridays will commence instead at Monks Eleigh (Lion) at 2.50 p.m.
The 12.45 p.m. journey from Sudbury to Bildeston on Weds. will terminate at Monks Eleigh (Lion).
The 4.35 p.m. journey from Halstead to Sudbury on Mondays and Wednesdays will be suspended.

SERVICE 17. Sudbury–Gestingthorpe–Yeldham–Braintree.
The 9.30 a.m. journey from Sudbury on Saturdays will be suspended, and 12.20 p.m. journey from Braintree will commence instead at Gestingthorpe (Foundry Corner) at 1.30 p.m.

SERVICE 19. Sudbury–Wickham St. Paul–Gestingthorpe–Belchamp–Sudbury.
The 11.10 a.m. journey from Sudbury on Thursdays and Saturdays will return from Gestingthorpe via the main road, omitting Wickham St. Paul, Catley Cross and Twinstead Cross Roads.
The 10.30 p.m. journey from Sudbury on Saturdays will omit Bulmer Village on the outward journey, and will return from Gestingthorpe via Bulmer Village, omitting Belchamp Walter and Borley.

SERVICE 21. Sudbury–Wickham St. Paul–Twinstead–Pebmarsh–Halstead.
The 3.40 p.m. journey from Sudbury on Mondays and Wednesdays will be suspended.
The 3.40 p.m. journey from Sudbury on Thursdays, and the 6.05 p.m. on Saturdays, will omit Twinstead Cross Roads.

SERVICE 22. Sudbury–Waldingfield–Acton–Lavenham.
The 10.35 p.m. journey from Sudbury on Sundays will be suspended.
The restriction applied to the 6.0 p.m. journey from Sudbury on Wednesdays will be removed.

SERVICE 23. Sudbury–Waldingfield–Acton–Sudbury.
The 10.20 p.m. journey from Acton to Sudbury on Wednesdays, and the 11.30 p.m. journey from Sudbury to Acton on Saturdays will be suspended.
The 7.45 a.m. journey from Acton to Sudbury on Mondays to Fridays will be withdrawn, and will be replaced by a journey at 7.0 a.m.

SPECIAL NOTICE REGARDING LONDON SERVICES.
In order to maintain the daily service to London, the Company has to exercise the greatest possible economy, and in particular to avoid running avoidable reliefs. Passengers are requested to assist in this by booking in advance wherever possible, and by stating the date and time of return when booking.

Clearly something had to be done and we were all granted an immediate increase in fares – which did our carryings no good. The Passenger Vehicle Operators Association (PVOA), of which we were members, sponsored a series of meetings and Bert and I went over to Kelvedon, where Harold Moore of Moore Bros. explained that there would have to be co-ordination of school contracts (which did not concern us) and a general cut-back of stage carriage mileage by 20 per cent. It was agreed that the cuts could wait until after Christmas, by which time the Suez crisis had become a disaster and the last British troops had been withdrawn.

I grew very depressed. Hungary weighed heavily on my mind, as a lover of liberty both for people and nations. I had failed to sell the house at Hadstock and the 70 miles a day car commuting was taking its toll – one Saturday night, after my usual double shift, I went to sleep at the wheel not far from home, fortunately with no serious consequences. Then, in the midst of all this, I found a buyer. We had looked at several houses in and around Sudbury, most of which would have been too expensive to run, but in late November I found a small pre-war detached property on the Melford Road, costing very little more than what I expected to get for 'Goldacre'. We moved to 'Redstacks' in the New Year.

I hated leaving Hadstock. The house had become part of me as no other ever has. I got a goose for Christmas from a friend of Snigley's at Little Yeldham and we lived off it right up to the move, feeding everyone soup made from the carcass on the day we left. The move was problematic, for because of petrol rationing the removers could only let us have one van, for one trip, so I took the 26-seater to shift the rest of the furniture after dark. Billy Bird and some of the other men came to help and everyone said how much better it would be for me to be nearer to my work. But I knew that I was leaving part of myself behind at Hadstock and part of my marriage too.

All the same, the move had to happen. We settled down and I could have my meals at home; Ena had been giving me lunch ever since she and Bert moved into the company's house at Acton. I soon grew to like Sudbury and the house, looking out over the water meadows, was pleasant and easy to run. I could concentrate once more on our problems and my wife on the prospective arrival of our second child.

Eastern National had introduced their service cuts early in January but we held on till the 28th. Some of the mileage we were quite glad to get rid of and most of the 20 per cent I found from small cuts here and there, the biggest single deletions being the 11.15 pm from London on Saturdays and the Saturday morning service to Braintree via Great Yeldham. But we also announced that we wanted to reduce the number of stopping places in villages like Gestingthorpe and our own home village at Acton. We probably lost more from increasing our fares than we saved from the mileage cuts, but no-one in the bus industry did well out of Suez.

Then too we had bad weather, if only briefly. Heavy snow one Wednesday left the London coach marooned in Stowmarket, where Charley Gilson spent the night at Ratcliffe's home. We tried to run the last journey on each route, which is good practice at such times, but we had to terminate the 6 pm from Kings Cross at Lavenham. On the Thursday Charley got home, but little else moved, though we got to Sudbury with the breakdown truck and fetched bread and milk for the shop at Acton. Later Snigley and I took the truck round the Gestingthorpe routes to see what sort of service we might run on the Friday and it was interesting to see how many of our regular passengers were walking to

Sudbury on market day, over distances of five miles and more. The truck was an ex-RAF desert rescue vehicle, very high off the ground and Snigley used its protruding hubs to skim a layer of snow off the banks as we went along, much to our satisfaction as the snow flew in all directions. We ran what we could on the Friday, including the London service and on the Saturday we were back to normal.

We had de-licensed the Rippingale 20-seater, BMR 690, at the start of the year and at the beginning of February we sold the other Rippingale bus and the 37-seater *Vega*. This eased the cash flow problem during the dead months of the year and demonstrated that we had been right to buy Bluffy's business. With BMR also sold in March we had reduced the combined fleet from 15 vehicles to ten; a good example of economies of scope, which I use in my economics lectures to this day. Word reached us from Cambridge that the Traffic Commissioners thought we were doing well – though this did not prevent them from imposing upon us a 'difficult' Vehicle Examiner, whom Alan Chinery had refused to admit to the premises.

Then an odd quirk of licensing procedure turned up. We had an excursion to Layer Road for home matches of Colchester United FC, the "U's", so we decided to advertise it, along with a similar destination on the Rippingale group. Straight away Max Chambers was on the phone, saying that we could not run from Sudbury itself, because Chambers had successfully objected to the Sudbury picking-up point when Corona had applied to add the destination to the licence. I checked the document and found no such restriction. Then the Commissioners' office wrote and phoned, saying that the restriction had been omitted by oversight (egg-on-face department), so would we (1) refrain from picking up at Sudbury and (2) send them the licence for endorsement. To the first request we had to agree, because one does not wilfully flout such a request from the licensing authority, but to the second I said no.

The result was a 'proposal to vary', published in Notices & Proceedings, to which we duly lodged an objection. Bert and I went to the public hearing which followed and so did the Chambers brothers, only to find that they had no *locus standi* and so could not be heard. The new chairman, Mr. Ormond, overruled us in favour of his officials, despite their error and we had to forget football. It did the local fans no good; they still had to get to Colchester by Chambers' bus and catch a Corporation bus to Layer Road, while we were never able to get a load up from the villages without the Sudbury traffic. But when I hear of a Colchester win I still shout, "Up the U's!".

On 15 March my second son was born at my wife's parents' home in Cambridge. I had warned Bert that I would be off at short notice when the time came and that morning the old Austin made record time, getting me there so as to assist at the birth. My home life had become a bit more leisured now, though my wife was not happy with the commitment I was giving to the business, which she said prevented her making any friends. We had had a holiday in the Cotswolds in the autumn of 1956, taking the Humber car, but I had been on the phone to Bert each evening we were away. A partnership in business is every bit as demanding as a partnership in marriage and happy are they who can combine both.

Running the business

There followed a fairly routine period during which I was working on further revisions to the local services. The temporary increase in the fuel tax was removed and our fares

PROGRAMME OF
EXCURSIONS and TOURS by LUXURY COACH
for CHRISTMAS and the NEW YEAR

1. **SUDBURY & DISTRICT.** Picking up at Lavenham, Great and Little Waldingfield, Acton, Long Melford and Sudbury, and as indicated below.

Day and Date	Depart Sudbury	Destination	Return fare Adult	Child	Notes
Sat, 6th Dec	2C20 pm	COLCHESTER for shopping, &c	3/6	2/8	C
Wed, 10th Dec	8.30 am	EARLS COURT Smithfield Show	12/6	8/6	A
	8.30 am	OLYMPIA Nat. Poultry Show	12/6	8/6	A
Sat, 13th Dec	8.30 am	LONDON—King's Cross	10/-	6/9	A
	12.45 pm	IPSWICH FOOTBALL	3/6	2/3	B
Wed, 17th Dec	10.0 am	CAMBRIDGE for shopping, &c	6/-	4/-	B
Fri, 19th Dec	8.30 am	LONDON—King's Cross	10/-	6/9	AB
Sat, 20th Dec	10.0 am	NORWICH for shopping, &c	7/6	4/9	B
	12.45 pm	IPSWICH FOOTBALL	3/6	2/3	B
Fri, 26th Dec	12.45 pm	IPSWICH FOOTBALL	3/6	2/3	B
Sat, 27th Dec	3.30 pm	IPSWICH PANTOMIMES 5.0 pm performances	3/6	2/3	
Wed, 31st Dec	1.0 pm	BERTRAM MILLS CIRCUS at Olympia, 4.50 pm performance	12/6	8/6	A
Sat, 3rd Jan	6.30 pm	IPSWICH PANTOMIMES 8.0 pm performances	3/6	2/3	
Wed, 7th Jan	3.30 pm	HOLIDAY ON ICE at Wembley 7 45 p.m. performance	13/6	9/-	A

Key to Notes

A...Picks up at Bulmer Tye, Twinstead Cross Roads, Catley Cross, Maplestead 'Cock' and Maplestead 'Pump'

B...Picks up also at Monks Eleigh and Brent Eleigh.

C...Time at Long Melford (not picking up in Sudbury).

2. **CLARE & DISTRICT.** Picking up at Fenstead End, Thurston End, Clare, Cavendish & Glemsford, Stansfield & Poslingford.

Day and Date	Depart time from Clare	Cav'dish	Glems'd	Destination	Return fare Adult	Child
Sat, 6th Dec	2.0 pm	2.5	2.10	COLCHESTER shopping	4/3	2/9
Wed, 10th Dec			8.10	SMITHFIELD SHOW Earls Court	12/6	8/6
				POULTRY Show Olympia	12/6	8/6
Sat, 13th Dec	8.0 am	8.5	8.10	LONDON—King's Cross	8/3	5/6
	12.20 pm	12.25	12.30	IPSWICH FOOTBALL	4/6	3/-
				Fare from GLEMSFORD is—4/-		2/9
Fri, 19th Dec	8.0 am	8.5	8.10	LONDON—King's Cross	8/3	5/6
Sat, 20th Dec	9.30 am	9.35	9.40	NORWICH, shopping, &c	8/-	5/6
	12.20 pm	12.25	12.30	IPSWICH FOOTBALL	4/6	3/-
				Fare from GLEMSFORD is—4/-		2/9
Fri, 26th Dec	12.20 pm	12.25	12 30	IPSWICH FOOTBALL	4/6	3/-
				Fare from GLEMSFORD is—4/-		2/9
Sat, 27th Dec	3.0 pm	3.5	3.10	IPSWICH PANTOMIMES	4/6	3/-
				Fare from GLEMSFORD is—4/-		2/9
Wd, 31st Dec			12.40	BERTRAM MILLS CIRCUS Olympia, 4.50 pm	12/6	8/6
Sat, 3rd Jan	6.0 pm	6.5	6.10	IPSWICH PANTOMIMES	4/6	3/-
				Fare from GLEMSFORD is—4/-		2/9
Wed, 7th Jan			3.10	HOLIDAY ON ICE, Wembley	13/6	9/-

Excursions will also run from **GESTINGTHORPE & DISTRICT** as follows:

Tuesday, 16th December, to IPSWICH, leave Gestingthorpe 9.0 am
Fare 5/-, Children 3/6

Saturday, 27th December, to IPSWICH PANTOMIMES, leave Gestingthorpe 3.10 pm Fare 4/-, Children 2/9

EXCURSIONS RETURN AT THE FOLLOWING TIMES:
Colchester **5.30** Poultry Show **5.0** Smithfield Show **5.30** London (King's Cross) **6.0** Cambridge **6.0** Norwich **6.0** other excursions at end of match or performance.

𝕿𝖍𝖊 𝕯𝖎𝖗𝖊𝖈𝖙𝖔𝖗𝖘 𝖆𝖓𝖉 𝕾𝖙𝖆𝖋𝖋 𝖔𝖋 𝕮𝖔𝖗𝖔𝖓𝖆 𝕮𝖔𝖆𝖈𝖍𝖊𝖘 join in wishing all who travel on the Company's services 𝕬 𝕸𝖊𝖗𝖗𝖞 𝕮𝖍𝖗𝖎𝖘𝖙𝖒𝖆𝖘 𝖆𝖓𝖉 𝕬 𝕳𝖆𝖕𝖕𝖞 𝖆𝖓𝖉 𝕻𝖗𝖔𝖘𝖕𝖊𝖗𝖔𝖚𝖘 𝕹𝖊𝖜 𝖄𝖊𝖆𝖗.

1958

CORONA COACHES LIMITED
Head Office and Travel Agency:
OLD MARKET PLACE, SUDBURY, SUFFOLK
Telephone: Sudbury 2193

Holiday Traffic Arrangements - Christmas 1958

Christmas Eve, Wednesday, December 24th

SERVICE 1. LONDON - SUDBURY - STOWMARKET. Normal Wednesday service, with additional journeys at 2.0 pm from London to Stowmarket, & at 9.15 pm from London to Sudbury

,, 1A. LONDON - SUDBURY - HADLEIGH. Normal Wednesday Service.

,, 4. LONDON - SUDBURY - REDE (connecting for BURY ST. EDMUNDS) Normal Wednesday Service

,, 11. SUDBURY - MELFORD - LAVENHAM - BILDESTON - STOWMARKET Normal **Thursday** Service

,, 12. CLARE - STANSFIELD - REDE - BURY ST. EDMUNDS Normal Wednesday Service

,, 13. CAVENDISH - GLEMSFORD - REDE - BURY ST. EDMUNDS Normal Wednesday Service

,, 15. CLARE - CAVENDISH - GLEMSFORD - SUDBURY Normal **Thursday** Service

,, 17. SUDBURY - GESTINGTHORPE - YELDHAM BRAINTREE (connecting for BLACK NOTLEY HOSPITAL) Normal Wednesday Service

,, 18. GESTINGTHORPE - LT. YELDHAM - SUDBURY Normal **Thursday** Service

,, 19. SUDBURY - GESTINGTHORPE - SUDBURY. Normal **Thursday** Service, except that the 1.0 pm journey from Henny to Sudbury and the 3.20 pm return to Henny **will not run**

,, 21. SUDBURY - TWINSTEAD - PEBMARSH - HALSTEAD Normal **Monday** Service, with an additional journey at 4.35 pm from Halstead (The Swan) to Sudbury via direct route

,, 22. SUDBURY - LAVENHAM - BILDESTON - STOWMARKET Normal **Thursday** Service

,, 23. SUDBURY - ACTON - SUDBURY. Normal **Thursday** Service, except that the 4.0 pm from Sudbury to Acton **will not run**

,, 30. GLEMSFORD - SUDBURY - HEDINGHAM. Normal Wednesday Service

,, 31. HEDINGHAM - YELDHAM - CLARE. Normal Wednesday Service

CHRISTMAS DAY
ALL SERVICES SUSPENDED

Boxing Day, Friday, December 26th

SERVICES 1, 1A & 4. LONDON - STOWMARKET. HADLEIGH and REDE (for BURY ST. EDMUNDS.) Normal Friday Services

,, 11 & 22. SUDBURY - LAVENHAM - BILDESTON STOWMARKET. The following *Special Service* will be operated :—
Depart Stowmarket 8.30 am and 4.45 pm for Sudbury
,, ,, 9.30 pm for Lavenham
,, Sudbury 12 nn., 7.30 & 8.50 pm for Stowmarket

SERVICE 12. CLARE - STANSFIELD - REDE - BURY ST. EDMUNDS. The following *Special Service* will be operated :
Depart Bury St. Eds. 8.45 am, 1.10 & 6.10 pm for Clare
,, Clare 12.20 & 5.10 pm for Bury St. Edmunds

,, 15. CLARE - CAVENDISH - GLEMSFORD SUDBURY Normal *Sunday* Service

All other local services will be suspended on Boxing Day.

See overleaf for Holiday Excursion Programme

We shall be happy to help you with all your travel problems

Daily Service to London

1958

41

CORONA COACHES LTD

PROGRAMME OF EXCURSIONS AND TOURS BY LUXURY COACH, DECEMBER, 1957, TO JANUARY, 1958.

Excursions from Sudbury and District.

Destination	Fare Adult	Child	Depart Sudbury	Return Time	Dates of Operation
CAMBRIDGE New Square	5/6	3/9	10.00 a.m.	6.00 p.m.	Wed. 11th Dec. 1957
COLCHESTER Bus Park	3/0	2/0	2.00 p m ✖	6.00 p m	Sat 14th Dec, 1957
✖—Time at Lavenham (does not pick up at Sudbury)					Sat., 21st Dec., 1957
LONDON King's Cross	10/0	6/9	8.00 a.m.	6.00 p.m.	Fri., 13th Dec., 1957
					Fri., 20th Dec., 1957
NORWICH Bell Avenue	7/6	5/0	10.00 a.m.	6.00 p.m.	Sat., 14th Dec., 1957
					Wed., 18th Dec., 1957
					Sat., 18th Jan., 1958
THE SMITHFIELD SHOW ... Earl's Court	12/6	8/3	8.00 a.m.	5.30 p.m.	Wed., 4th Dec., 1957
NATIONAL POULTRY SHOW .. Olympia	12/6	8/3	8.00 a.m.	5.00 p.m.	Wed., 4th Dec., 1957

PANTOMIMES, ICE SHOWS and CIRCUSES (For picking up times, enquire when booking.)

TOM ARNOLD'S CIRCUS (Harringay)—Friday, 10th January, 1958.
Fare: Adults 10/-, Children 6/9.
BERTRAM MILLS CIRCUS (Olympia)—Wednesday 1st January, 1958.
Fare: Adults 12/6, Children 8/3,
"WINTER WONDERLAND" ICE SHOW (Wembley)—Wednesday, 8th January, 1958.
Fare: Adults 13/6, Children 9/0.
"ALADDIN" (Colchester Repertory)—Thursdays, 2nd and 16th January, 1958.
"SINBAD THE SAILOR" (Colchester Hippodrome)—Thursdays 2nd and 16th January, 1958
Fare: Adults 3/0, Children 2/0.

Theatre, &c. Tickets available through our Agents and Offices when you book your Coach seats.

Excursions from Gestingthorpe and District.

Destination	Fare Adult	Child				Return Time	Date of Operation
COLCHESTER Bus Park	3/0	2/0	...	...	...	6.00 p.m.	Sat., 14th Dec., 1957
IPSWICH Half Moon and Star ..	5/0	3/3	...	...	...	4.00 p.m.	Tues. 10th Dec., 1957
							Tues. 17th Dec., 1957

Coaches will also run from Gestingthorpe and District to Sudbury to connect with the following excursions
(Additional Fare 2/0 return, Children 1/3.)

LONDON King's Cross (13th and 20th Dec.); NORWICH (Sat., 14th Dec.) SMITHFIELD and POULTRY SHOWS (Wed., 4th Dec.) BERTRAM MILLS CIRCUS (Wed., 1st Jan.) "WINTER WONDERLAND" (Wed., 8th Jan.) TOM ARNOLD'S CIRCUS (Friday, 10th January)

A Coach will also run from Gestingthorpe and District on Thursdays 2nd and 16th January, for "ALADDIN," at Colchester Repertory, and "SINBAD THE SAILOR" at Colchester Hippodrome Fare 3/0, (Children 2/0.)

DAY RETURNS TO LONDON are available every day by regular service coach. Return at 6.00 p,m., Mondays to Fridays; 11.15 p,m., Saturdays, and 8.15 p.m., Sundays.

May we draw your attention to the following special events which may be conveniently visited by using our Express Services : Schoolboy's Own Exhibition (London, 31st December to 11th January); Inter-Varsity Rugger (Twickenham, 10th December).

Further details, and Bookings, from our Agents in all the villages served, or Head Office,
OLD MARKET PLACE, SUDBURY. Telephone 2193.

went down, but by no means all of the Suez cuts were replaced (the two principal ones were). The petrol ration had become a farce by the time the government announced a 50 per cent increase for Easter and in April we were forced to put our fares up again. Each time we did this I made a point of conducting each duty in turn and explaining the need to ask for more from our customers; this certainly cushioned the effect of the increase, but we lost traffic just the same. We knew our passengers well enough to learn who had bought a car or a moped, or who was being given a lift by the local farmer's wife. What we saw also was the sale of cottages for second homes, which sometimes meant another weekender on the London service but more often just more lost traffic on the local buses.

Sometimes though, the cottages just disappeared. Conducting the local services gave me time to talk and watch and sometimes the drivers would say "There used to be a couple of cottages there", pointing to what was now the edge of a ploughed field. The local *clunch* soon decays and another landmark is gone as if it had never been. The drivers missed little; Charley Gilson told me that he had watched the fields over the years he had been driving the London coach and he had seen their colour grow steadily lighter, as the farmers took more out and put less back in. Not that the men felt any affection for the land: the countryman's attitude to it was summed up for me one evening in the 'Crown', at Acton. Conversation turned to football pools and Snigley was asked what he would do if he won. "I'd buy forty acres o' land", he said, with feeling, "And I'd conkareet the lot. Then that'd be no more trouble to nobody".

John Foley Egginton got in touch that spring and suggested that I had a go at a prize competition being organised by the Institute of Traffic Administration (now the Institute of Transport Administration). The subject was *Costing in the Motor Bus Industry* and I obtained second prize, though I think my essay must have been pretty primitive by the standards of today - as indeed was so much of the industry's costing. It surprises me now, looking back, how little we knew about our financial performance; or perhaps I was too busy and Bert did not want to tell me. I just concentrated on getting more out of our vehicles and staff.

Each day as I typed the orders ready to be taken to Acton on the 5 o'clock bus I would get through a pile of cigarettes, without really noticing. I had already been warned about the dangers of smoking, but the pile of butt-ends made me think it was rather a waste of money, so I gave up; rather to Bert's annoyance since he smoked as heavily as I did. The daily orders formed the centre of the day's work for me and in the summer the weekends needed to be planned well in advance. The London drivers would bring a note of the bookings on the charts at Kings Cross and our own charts gave some guidance, but there was always an element of guesswork about passengers who did not pre-book. The excursion charts needed to be carefully monitored, for profit margins were tight and a full load on a 38-seater could easily become a loss if I decided to 'let it run' and then failed to fill two 29s.

Saturday meant doing two days'

orders, so my conducting duty that brought me into the office from time to time was vital. Eventually I would be away at five, conducting the relief to the 2 o'clock from London, taking local traffic as far as Lavenham, where there was 40 minutes layover before bringing the 'picture bus' back at 6.15. As I remember it was usually Snigley driving and while he turned the bus I would go into Mr. Fisk's shop (he was also the booking agent) and buy the grapefruit for Sunday breakfast. Those and my ticket machine went onto the luggage rack out of sight (but the cash bag I kept) and Snigley and I would go into the back bar of the 'Swan', for half a pint and a game of darts. There was a tacit understanding on such occasions that you only bought a half, so that the driver could keep face by buying one back and neither drank too much. There was trust in those days, now alas long lost. The cash bag gave my throw a peculiar tilt and so did the low ceiling; sad to say the back bar has long since been turned into more superior accommodation and the 'Swan' no longer caters for busmen. Back at Old Market Place there was time to go home for a meal, and then we would cover the 9.10 and 10.30 trips on the Gestingthorpe circular, finishing a long day at 11.25 pm. Yet all the time there was the feeling of being among friends - the staff, the passengers; you need never be never alone in a country bus business.

With the spring came more changes. We felt we needed to improve the fleet and one day when I was conducting Bert on a Halstead duty he explained how he thought we could afford a new vehicle, provided I could manage without the 33-seat *Vega*. This would leave us with only the 38-seater as a traditional luxury coach, for the 29-seater *Vistas* were getting a bit elderly, but we felt we ought to buy something specifically for the London service, where our principal source of revenue lay. The result was KGV 195, a dual-purpose machine designed with our special needs in mind; an AEC *Reliance* with a bus-style Burlingham body. It was a sort of square tube with standard segments, into which were placed 41 full luxury coach seats. As a final touch Bert had the idea of specifying seats intended for a 7' 6" body (KGV being 8' 0") and having them set back from the sides. This gave a bit of extra space for the passenger on the inside seat to spread into, which was in

BELOW: KGV 195 again, resting at Kings Cross coach station having worked the morning journey from Stowmarket. *(Essex Bus Group)*

fact noticed and appreciated and also avoided the discomfort that comes from sitting too close to the skin of the coach on a cold day. We caused a great deal of comment by specifying scrapers instead of ashtrays on the backs of the seats - ashtrays are horrible things that get full of toffee papers, apple cores and even razor blades and they have to be turned onto the floor, so why not let all the stuff go onto the floor in the first place?

In effect KGV was a coach for the long-distance passengers and a bus for the traffic at the country end. We were very proud of it, but Alan and Mrs. Chinery thought we were fools not to have bought a full luxury coach with an eye to the private hire trade. They may have been right, but we saw the London service as our bread and butter and felt that its requirements should come first. Jokey drove the new machine most, but on Thursdays it was brought in for maintenance in the morning and used on the busy market-day services in the afternoon.

KGV arrived in June 1957 at about the same time as we introduced our first set of service revisions. These involved separating Stowmarket–Sudbury from Sudbury–Halstead (except for the through London journeys) and adding some more local mileage. Mrs. Chinery had pointed out that the village of Preston St. Mary, near Lavenham, had never seen a bus service, so we diverted certain journeys on 'the doddle'. At the same time we had to make a significant change to the positioning journeys on Service 1.

Ratcliffe, the London conductor whose home was in Stowmarket decided to retire and we found an excellent replacement in Tom Tobin, a man who lived locally. This meant that the morning journey to Stowmarket and the late night return could be scheduled as stage carriage, which simplified the fare table. But it also meant that on Mondays to Fridays we had a nasty 'split end', requiring two men from 9.10pm to 11.15pm, usually at overtime rates. To save expense Bert and I got into the habit of covering it ourselves, either together or with one of the other men, often giving us time for a drink together at the 'Two Sisters' at Stowmarket. But it was not my idea of the ideal night out - each coach had to be filled up and checked before finishing the duty and my job was to sweep out (hence my dislike of ashtrays).

We had our occasional problems, such as the Sunday evening when four men, all well gone in drink, tried to board

the 7.30 pm London coach at Old Market Place. I kept them talking by the near side of the vehicle while one of the drivers shut the door and gave Bert the sign to pull away. When they realised what had happened they were not well pleased and for my part I was not sorry when the three drivers - two from the feeder coaches and Billy Bird, who was about to leave on the doddle – quietly ranged themselves alongside me. We had been well within our rights in refusing to carry them and finally they disappeared in the direction of the railway station, where no doubt Mr. Postle was well able for them.

Tom was an immediate success as the London conductor and none of the other men grudged standing in for him on the

Service		Pence per car-mile (pcm) Week ending		
		12.5.57	28.4.58	11.5.58
11	Stowmarket–Halstead	5.93	7.83	8.10
16	Sudbury–Ipswich	9.44	7.94	15.73
17	Sudbury–Braintree	9.31	20.83	17.02
18	Gestingthorpe Circular	19.78	14.47	20.68
19	Gestingthorpe Circular	17.17	22.16	17.44
20	Sudbury–Halstead	16.21	17.86	11.23
21	Sudbury–Halstead	8.65	6.80	10.30
22	Sudbury–Stowmarket*	23.14	14.92	15.36
23	Sudbury–Acton Circular	6.54	10.44	11.62
29	Sudbury–Maplestead	n/a	n/a	24.00

STAGE SERVICES – COSTS AND REVENUE 1957 - 1958

* 'The Doddle'

Average movement cost. 1958 - 10.5 pcm
Average total cost, 1958 - 18.25 pcm

occasional winter Saturday when he would ask for his rest day to be changed to that he could go up on the service to watch Leyton Orient – "such devotion!", they would say, with a smile. One day when I had a streaming cold Tom came into the office and offered me what he described as 'some medicine' from a flask produced from his greatcoat pocket. Not to be outfaced in front of him and the others I knocked back the contents of the flask cap and when I had done spluttering I asked him that the so-and-so it was. "A mixture of black-current juice and 120 per cent Polish spirit", he said and I said no-one had better strike a match anywhere near me for awhile. But it cured my cold and I am sure Tom was glad of it many times, out on the road in winter. Sad, that it would be prohibited today.

Tom was but one example of the way we recruited staff. I think that in fact there was a sort of waiting list; certainly we had only to lose a man for heads to be put together and then someone - usually Bill Swindells and Billy Bird - would come into the office and it would be, "If you want someone we could have a word with so-and-so", which meant they had done so already. We never had anything to complain about the men who joined us with such a recommendation. Both Bert and I worked on an 'open door' principle (as I have ever since); my office at Sudbury was open house, unless Maude had been told to ensure my privacy, for staff and customers and, for that matter, for competitors too.

The summer months meant excursion traffic and the programme had

BELOW: Taken at a later date (16 July 1972, at Llangollen), here we see (third from left) Billy Bird, the Shop Steward. (Source unknown)

to be planned in advance. I found a cheap local printer to produce a monthly leaflet and we advertised in the *Free Press* every week, winter and summer, always at the same corner of the same page. We also developed the travel agency side of the business, adding a facility for booking seats in the London theatres. Our idea was that in due course the net revenue from this would cover the overheads of the Sudbury office. Much later on John Niblock of Eastern Counties was instrumental in getting us a sub-agency for London Coastal Coaches so that we could book on all the main express coach services, but for the moment we were more limited. Even so, we took a full page advertisement in the local paper which paid for itself as we resold space to firms whose services we *could* book on, such as Grey Green and Premier Travel.

Changes continued. Gordon Clampin came in one day and apologetically gave in his notice. He was leaving, he said, to work for Chambers, where he would be on a regular bus service rota and better able to plan his family life and his wife was growing tired of working as a part-time conductor. Some people prefer a predictable series of duties, while others are happier with the more varied life of a business such as ours. And some preferred, in those days, the security they expected from a 'territorial' company such as Eastern National.

Of our two neighbours it was more often Eastern Counties with whom we had dealings, despite the fact that their headquarters lay far away in Norwich. That meant that I had little to do with Harry Vincent, the Clacton District Traffic Superintendent for Eastern National, who was an interesting man to talk to. He told me that once, in Tilling days, Sir Frederick Heaton (the chairman) himself visited the Clacton office and told Harry that in future all financial and statistical reports were to be copied to him, the envelope to be addressed to him and to carry a red star (which he was to go and buy from a stationer so that they reached him personally. We wondered at this approach to management by the chairman of a great

combine, who wanted to see depot figures from one of so many subsidiary companies. Harry went on to become Area Traffic Superintendent at Colchester, retiring in 1967 and I have often felt that men like him and Bill Hall at Norwich stayed too long in traffic positions, so that their experience was never brought into the field of general management.

Stormclouds gather

We had only had KGV in service for about a month when the next blow fell. Platform staff in the big bus companies were organised by the Transport & General Workers Union (T&GWU), except for some areas where the National Union of Railwaymen had inherited this function. In those days there was a 'national agreement' governing pay and conditions of service, which the Passenger Vehicle Operators Association (PVOA) had carefully avoided. Most small firms tend to resist organisation by a Union, but Corona had its own agreement (conveniently, it had not actually been signed by either side). Anyway, Bert and I encouraged Union membership, pointing out that the Union would help with any court proceedings which we could not afford, however much we might wish to. Union branch meetings were held in the public bar of the 'White Horse' at Sudbury, round the corner from the office and then Bert and I would sit in the snug so as to be accessible for negotiation. It really worked very well.

The working agreement which thus existed paid off when, on 20 July 1957, the T&GWU brought the provincial busmen out for an additional pound a week. That was the first (and so far the only) national bus strike; the 'Coronation strike' of 1937 was discouraged in the provinces by Ernie Bevin, who was using it as a stick to beat the syndicatist busmen in London. On the first morning Billy Bird came over to me outside the running sheds and asked, "Guv'ner, are we parties to the dispute?" (correctly accenting the word on the first syllable). "You know we're not", I said. "Can I have the Austin, then?" Without a word I chucked

BELOW: KGV 195 from the rear; the AEC Reliance with Burlingham 41-seat body, which we bought for the London service - note full luxury seating in what was manifestly a bus. *(Author's collection)*

over the keys and off he went to Halstead. There he found the Eastern National men getting ready to stop the independents running, but when Billy explained our position to his opposite number they decided to leave the Corona alone and stop Blackwells instead. (Later there was some unpleasantness at Colchester North Station, when the Chambers brothers tried a bit of strike-breaking).

Billy's intervention saved us and his members from a lot of grief. We had Eric on the phone, worried about insurance and he said he would have a word with a friend of his in the Essex police. Later we were told that a police car followed each journey on the London service through the county, out of sight but near enough to be on the scene if there were trouble. We just hoped they did not clock our actual running speed, often well over the then legal limit of 30 miles an hour.

The strike did us no good, though. Many passengers took it for granted that we would not be running, while others were unable to reach our coaches and the London service lost a lot of traffic; you don't get that sort of traffic back easily. On 24 July the companies made an offer of 11/- (55p) an hour which was accepted and their men went back the next day. As we had promised to do, we passed the same increase to our own staff.

The summer saw us busy on all sides. Bert and I could no longer take alternate Sundays off; he was driving on one of the busiest days of the week and I was in charge at Old Market Place. Excursion and private hire bookings were brisk and so far no-one had a better standard of vehicle than ours, though we knew that Jack Mulley was getting new under-floor engined coaches which would make all the local fleets look out of date. (Two years later you could buy a second-hand AEC Regal III half-cab for £300). However, there was little time to think and for me each day built up to the typing of the next day's orders and each night built up to waking in the small hours afraid I had left something out – a fear that still disturbs my sleep at times, more than 40 years later.

We kept our wider interests as far as we could. We agreed that Bert would represent our interests with PSV Operators Ltd, the company that ran the Kings Cross Coach Station and managed a chain of booking agents, while I would do the same with the PVOA. This in due course brought me on to the National Council and to become vice chairman of the London & Home Counties Committee (in time to lean heavily against the idea of licensing private hire operation). We were both members of the Institute of Transport, but we had no time to get to their meetings. In the winter of 1957-1958 I did my first bit of lecturing, to a Workers Education Association group at Great Henny, on the history of transport.

But the year was not to end without more trouble. The nation's finances lurched from *Stop* to *Go* with horrible regularity and when they were at *Go* the limits came off hire-purchase and our passengers bought cars and motor cycles. But that autumn the *Stop* sign went up and on 19 September Bank Rate went up from five to seven per cent, along with a sharp squeeze on credit. Coming at the end of the season, with the thin months ahead, we had to meet it in the only way open to us, so as to meet the requirements of a friendly bank manager and on 30 October we raised all local service fares; the London fares having gone up along with all other express operators' fares on the first of that month.

As if that were not enough, the government decided to end national service. One source of revenue we had budgeted for had been the leave service every three weeks from RAF Wattisham. On 'long weekends' the up coaches on Friday could provide reliefs from London on the Saturday morning and the return leg could be covered by reliefs on the up

journey on Sunday, so the whole operation should have been very rewarding. In fact we ran no more than two or three times, so the prospect of losing the traffic with the phasing out of national service should not have worried us too much, though we had always hoped. We knew that Jack Mulley had taken the odd load from the far side of the runway, paying no commission to the authorities at the airfield and we knew that several other firms were doing the same, charging a good deal less than our licensed fares. Without proof there was little we could do, and we were doubtful as to the wisdom of trying to get that proof by cloak-and-dagger work. Overall, though, it was clear that a good deal of revenue we had expected was not coming in.

Wheeling and dealing

The Wattisham business left us feeling that Jack Mulley was the joker in the pack. Our other competitors were either too small or were people we could negotiate with; Jack had a reputation as a sharp customer, though he was clearly a good operator. Snigley said to me once, "That Mister Mulley, he'd remind you of one of the old farmers, they kept good 'orses" and it was true that his fleet was always well turned out. He was feared, though, by those of the West Suffolk firms that were not in some way his clients. That winter we felt his influence close at hand.

In November we had a visit from Wilfred Cooper. Standing in the back office at Sudbury he told us he was thinking of selling the business he had inherited from his father, based at Combs, south of Stowmarket. There was a local bus service that ran daily from the Wattisham area into Stowmarket, a less frequent one to Ipswich and a one-third share in the RAF leave service. We decided to have a look at it. Bert was given sight of such records as were available and I roughed out some car workings. Apart from feeding in a bit of traffic from the villages to the London service at Hitcham there was little in it for us and it would not offer the economies of scope we had obtained from the Rippingale services. The private hire business we knew we could write off. So, despite a second visit from Wilfred when he more or less threatened to sell to Jack Mulley, we decided to let the offer pass.

On 1 December short period licences to replace Cooper's services were issued to a new firm called Combs Coaches Limited, whose address, High Street, Ixworth, was that of Mulleys Motorways Limited. We knew Wilfred had done the only thing he could, despite his clear preference for selling his business to us. We knew, too, that we had been right to refuse him. I put my car graphs away and concentrated on the Christmas traffic. When KGV was involved in an accident in the Mile End Road I had enough to worry me, but the unit structure of the Burlingham body made repairs (or replacement, rather; a new front end was put on) straightforward and Bakers had the coach back on the road for the seasonal peak.

With the New Year our attention turned to the north and we decided we ought to get into Bury St. Emunds. I think I was less enthusiastic than Bert, but there was potential for traffic to and from the A12 road into London and Eastern Counties only served the route in the summer. We decided to apply for the Hartest service to start from Bury, coming out through the village of Rede. At the same time we had a shot at getting back some of the Halstead traffic we had lost when we altered the timings; south of the town we followed a different route to Eastern National, so we applied for stages at Blamsters Crescent, a housing estate and Pennypot, a hamlet slightly further south.

The traffic court case took up most of my time for some weeks and despite the cost of retaining Counsel the outcome was a bitter disappointment. It proved almost impossible to get anyone from Bury itself to give 'evidence of need' and it was probably a mistake to divide our efforts by bringing the Halstead issue up at all. In the decision we were allowed a picking-up point at Pennypots, which never produced more than the odd passenger, but we failed to get into Bury. Even worse, our witnesses from the villages were good enough to ensure that the Commissioners gave us an extension to start at Rede, which added quite a lot of really unremunerative mileage, including double working. I was hesitant about accepting the grant, but Bert convinced me that we ought to hold on to what we had been given so as to gave another go at Bury later on. In the meantime, Rede was a loss-maker and Maude composed a slightly naughty set of verses that started-

> *There was a young lady of Rede*
> *Who travelled by bus at great speed*

Very soon we were presented with an opportunity. Fred Honeywood had a small business based at Stanstead, just off our Hartest route, with a daily service from Glemsford to Bury and a workmen's and market-day one to Sudbury. His fleet was elderly to the point of eccentricity - he had recently been persuaded to sell back to Leyland for their museum the last petrol-engined double-decker in service, which he had bought from heaven knows where. Now, like Wilfred Cooper, Fred wanted to sell and Jack Mulley was once more in the background, Fred's presence in the back office was in marked contrast to the tall, rather gaunt figure of Wilfred Cooper. He told us he had an offer for his business from Goldsmith's of Sicklesmere, a firm that seemed to enjoy an ambiguous relationship with Jack, in that no-one knew whether they were on good terms or not (which doubtless suited Jack very well). It was Jack, Fred told us, who was pressing him to sell to Goldsmiths and thus raised our suspicions, specially when, a few days later, Jack himself dropped in and said he thought we ought to buy! Anyway, I got my graphs out again and once again there was no way I could justify the deal, while even the chance of getting into Bury St. Edmunds by the back door had been pre-empted by our policy over the Rede extension. When Bert saw the figures and looked over the fleet we just had to say no; apart from anything else there was no hope of getting a decent price for the rolling stock, even if I could have made the savings in car mileage. But I shall not forget the disappointment in Fred Honeywood's face when we had to tell him. Early in March Goldsmiths took over the business.

Financially things were not too good that winter and I think we were both getting apprehensive. In December we made a slight saving by withdrawing (for the second time) the Saturday service on Rippingale's old route to Braintree. At the same time we abandoned the Gainsford End spur and introduced interchangeable return tickets with Jennings, who also served the Great Yeldham to Braintree section on Wednesdays. In the spring I had an inspiration one day when conducting round Gestingthorpe and saw how we could introduce a service from Grear Maplestead to Sudbury on a Saturday afternoon with a minimum additional mileage and so Service 29 was introduced on 3 May. Somehow I got a great deal of satisfaction out of that and the traffic justified it, too.

Meanwhile the routine of running the business continued. When the time came for a new stock of tickets to be ordered I had a word with the owner of the milk bar in North Street that many of us frequented and sold him an advertisement on the backs of our tickets that covered their cost. Bert met someone in the management of Rickards, the London luxury

TABLE NINE	Proposal for transfer of Blackwell's licence with modification Omitting certain timing points

SUMMER SERVICE (1 May to 31 October)

	M&FO	TWTh	Saturday		Sunday	
	am	am	am	pm	am	pm
LAVENHAM ..	7 30	—	—	—	7 30	—
SUDBURY ..	7 55	7 55	7 55	12 55	7 55	5 55
BURES ..	8 10	8 10	8 10	1 10	8 10	6 10
CHAPPEL ..	8 20	8 20	8 20	1 20	8 20	6 20
HALSTEAD ..	8 45	8 45	8 45	1 45	8 45	6 45
BRAINTREE..	9 05	9 05	9 05	2 05	9 05	7 05
LONDON ..	11 20	11 20	11 20	4 10	11 20	9 10

	MF	Saturday		Sunday	
	pm	pm	pm	am	pm
LONDON ..	6 30	2 00	6 30	9 00	6 30
BRAINTREE..	8 35	4 15	8 35	11 15	8 35
HALSTEAD ..	8 55	4 35	8 55	11 35	8 55
CHAPPEL ..	9 20	5 00	9 20	12 00	9 20
BURES ..	9 30	5 10	9 30	12 10	9 30
SUDBURY ..	9 45	5 25	9 45	12 25	9 45

WINTER SERVICE (1 November to 30 April)

	M&FO	TWTh	Saturday		Sunday	
	am	am	am	pm	am	pm
LAVENHAM ..	7 30	—	—	—	—	—
—						
SUDBURY ..	7 55	9 25	7 55	12 55	9 25	5 55
BURES ..	8 10	9 40	8 10	1 10	9 40	6 10
CHAPPEL ..	8 20	9 50	8 20	1 20	9 50	6 20
HALSTEAD ..	8 45	10 15	8 45	1 45	10 15	6 45
BRAINTREE..	9 05	10 35	9 05	2 05	10 35	7 05
LONDON ..	11 20	12 50	11 20	4 10	12 50	9 10

	TWTh	M&FO	Saturday		Sunday	
	pm	pm	pm	pm	am	pm
LONDON ..	6 00	6 30	2 00	6 30	9 00	6 30
BRAINTREE..	8 05	8 35	4 15	8 35	11 15	8 35
HALSTEAD ..	8 25	8 55	4 35	8 55	11 35	8 55
CHAPPEL ..	8 50	9 20	5 00	9 20	12 00	9 20
BURES ..	9 00	9 30	5 10	9 30	12 10	9 30
SUDBURY ..	9 15	9 45	5 25	9 45	12 25	9 45

Notes: M&FO - Mondays and Fridays MF - Mondays to Fridays TWTh - Tuesdays, Wednesdays and Thursdays

Restrictions: The same passenger not to be both taken up and set down on the same journey between Sudbury and Mount Bures inclusive.

The same passenger not to be both taken up and set down on the same journey between Chappel and Halstead inclusive.

No passenger to be taken up between Lavenham and Sudbury inclusive for setting down between Sudbury and Mount Bures inclusive.

The same passenger not to be both taken up and set down between Lavenham and Sudbury inclusive.

coach firm with the Royal Appointment and the royal Coat of Arms on the side; they were short of work at weekends, so we started to hire them for Friday evening reliefs from Kings Cross. On the Saturday they worked on our local services, with our own conductresses to show the drivers the way and on the Sunday morning the men cleaned up and worked back relief to

ABOVE: GV 5063, new to Long in 1937, on Sudbury Market Hill in the post-war years. *(Essex Bus Enthusiasts Group)*

London in the evening. Two comments have remained in my mind, the first being that the drivers found it harder work round the lanes than they were used to in London. The second went to the heart of rural bus operation: a Rickards driver was working the Hadleigh service one Sunday evening and when he came into Old Market Place he said to me, "Funny thing about your passengers, Guv'ner – if yer stop fer an old cove by the roadside, he ain't goin' ter London and them that are'll be leanin' over a gate with their backs to yer". That was one thing that set us and Blackwell, Jennings and Premier, apart from our nationalised competitors – we could be expected to look after the individual customer.

But a lot of other things were starting to happen and it is true to say that they began to be too much for me so that my

BELOW: CCF 120, new to Long in 1949, comes through Long Melford working on hire to Corona in August 1956. *(Frank Church)*

health began to suffer. We decided there was money to be made by promoting tourist traffic out of London and Bert pointed out that we could do this legally by bringing people down on the London service and then using our excursion licence. We registered the trading name for this side of the business as *Gainsborough Tours* and had brochures printed for one-day inclusive tours from Kings Cross. These included an overall amount that covered the coach fare, the excursion, lunch at the 'Four Swans' at Sudbury and tea in the afternoon. One tour even included a boat trip on the River Orwell from Ipswich. The whole thing had the added attraction that we were able to include an on-cost to the catering element, so that the revenue per passenger was very good. After all, it cost virtually nothing to carry Gainsborough customers on the London service.

ABOVE: Long's *Vista* bodied MMP 915, outside the Glemsford depot, showing the A. J. Long logo. The business was recorded as 'E. F. Long, t/a A. J. Long'. *(Frank Church)*

BELOW: One of Long's double-deckers, DSG 168, an AEC Regent, loading on Market Hill at Sudbury in 1956 – the stands were later converted for use as a car park. *(Frank Church)*

No sooner had the Maplestead service got under way than Bert came in to say that he had met Syd Blackwell, who wanted to sell us his London service. No vehicles to be included; all he wanted was payment for the goodwill. Clearly we could not risk Eastern National getting hold of it and finally shutting us out of Halstead and Braintree and any way, it would effectively place us back where Chinery had been before the war in relation to that traffic. Here it seemed there was a really promising opening and we agreed terms at once. By the end of June we had our application published, for the transfer of the licence with modification.

I had concocted a scheme to break new ground. To escape dead mileage we would start the service from Lavenham, running though Sudbury and restoring the early morning up journey and the long day in London. But instead of covering the thin road to Halstead we would go through Great and Little Cornard and Bures, none of which had a service to London and cut access to Chappel, where Blackwell's route started. So as to keep the Halstead stage we would abandon the Coggeshall timings, which seemed sensible, since the Coggeshall traffic had had to move north to Earls Colne before turning west to Halstead and finally south to Braintree and London. Moore's bus service could bring Coggeshall people into Braintree and we could show the connection in our timetable. I proposed separate summer and winter schedules so as to allow for feeding traffic onto our existing timings when loadings might be poor and I felt rather proud of the whole scheme. The application included provision to protect Chambers between Sudbury and Bures, but of course it attracted immediate objections, from British Railways, Eastern National Eastern Counties and (for some unknown reason) Newton Secker Rule, our neighbour at Boxford.

In the midst of this we were made another offer which we felt we could not afford to refuse. Eddie Long suggested that we might buy his bus business, leaving him to run his haulage fleet. Here, from Clare to Sudbury, was a 'main road' route and one worked with double-deckers; in a way, it would make real operators of us. The fleet was elderly, but not to worry, it was kept busy and although there were not the possibilities for rationalisation that we had found with Rippingale, it would increase our turnover. We proposed to sell the older of Long's two AEC *Regals* and to do some refinancing, but even so we could not find the purchase price. Yet there was a further prize; services into Bury St. Edmunds that went through Rede. We might yet slip into Bury by the back door.

I had always got on well with Eddie and it was clear that he liked us and wanted us to have the business rather than anyone else (least of all Eastern National, who had once operated on the Clare road). So at our suggestion he agreed to take part payment in Corona shares and to join our Board. In the months that followed I was to be deeply grateful, for I found myself not just with a fellow-director but with a friend and just when I was to need one most.

After taking Eric's advice we went back to our accountants, and through them to Lombank, through whom we refinanced the combined fleets. I recall signing bills of exchange in their London office for what seemed like hours; bills which were to be presented thereafter with unfailing regularity. Bert and Eric signed them too. We were the more confident on account of the optimism of the accountants, who expected that we would make a surplus on the new business, over and above the capital repayment.

The chapter ends

I was plunged into it now. As well as running the traffic side and taking my share of the conducting duties I was preparing the licence applications, and spending a good deal of time with Eddie's manager, finding out just what his buses did. We also hatched up a scheme to get us into Bury by stealth, with Eddie's agreement. Before the licences were to be transferred he added certain journeys to his Clare-Bury licence that would in effect extend our service from Rede into the town. They made no traffic sense on their own, and I felt sure that they would be questioned by George Carruthers, the Eastern Counties Area Traffic Manager at Norwich, but in the event they went through without objection. We were ready to move in.

At Easter we had been hit once again by a trade dispute that was none of our business, when the London Transport busmen put in for a wage increase of 25s (£1.25) a week. Unsatisfied, they struck on 5 May and stayed out until 21 June. This probably did us more harm than the provincial busmen's strike of the previous year, because a good many of our London passengers reached the coach at places like Romford, using London Transport. (Indeed, at Romford the police and the planners had diverted all down journeys away from the Market Place, to pick up at a point well down Eastern Avenue from the bus stops, in a move I still find typical of the attitude of such people to public transport). In the middle of the strike I spent a week going to London each day to promote Gainsborough Tours, and at the suggestion of Bill Swindells I made a special point of calling on Shirley James, one of the pioneers of the coach business. Mr James remembered Bill, who had driven Corona vehicles on hire to Associated Motorways in the days when Shirley James was more involved with the operating side, and he left me with a very happy memory of that visit.

June was an exceptionally wet month and July and August were not much better. Revenue from private hire and excursions slumped - the weeks before the school holidays started were always a good time for that sort of traffic, with pub and club outings and good loads on our up-market tours. (That year we were advertising for the first time Stoneleigh Abbey and Coventry, with a stretch on the new M.1 motorway). Neither Bert nor I would admit it, but we were beginning to worry, and the strain was starting to tell. I had always suffered from hay fever, and that year it started to turn into asthma, while Bert had to see his doctor with a complaint about his feet. But the strain showed more in personal terms, in his relationship with both me and Eric. It worried him that for the time being the weight of the work was falling on me, but he was more aware than I was of the financial problems, and perhaps resented a certain lack of interest, or time, on my side, in that aspect of the business. But anyway, we were naive enough to convince ourselves that all had to go well so long as we were working so hard.

On 18 August 1958 we took over Eddie's fleet and started running his services. We set out quickly to repaint his dark blue and white in Corona colours and we altered the design of our fleet name for the double-deckers simply to read 'Corona'. We had decided to keep the fleet at Acton, despite the empty running; the Glemsford drivers all had cars and Bert felt, no doubt rightly, that we should share out the rotas and not risk any jealousies. We took on a carpenter to raise the roof of the running shed in the central bay so that we could get the 'deckers over the pit. Eddie's men soon mastered our ticket machines, with which we replaced his Bell Punch tickets (we had to order some weeklies, too), and Bert and I began to get to know the traffic.

It rained a lot. In fact, it was to be the wettest summer for many years, and there was not a wetter June until 1987. I remember conducting the 'circular'; the morning journey at seven o'clock from Glemsford into Sudbury, then on by way of Rippers' works at Sible Hedingham back to Clare, crossing the disused airfield at Ovington, and so back into Sudbury for the second time. This was real conducting, but I could see nothing through the wet windows of where we were, and where the stops are is something that the conductor needs to know. To get the feel of the traffic I put myself down to conduct each of the new duties, and, apart from my troubled breathing and a certain amount of stress in my private life I was in my element. I derived a certain satisfaction from the fact that we were now operating a bus service past Plumpton Hall, the home of Harley Drayton, chairman of British Electric Traction, and past Arthur Lainson's family home at Horringer.

Bert took his turn on some of the stage duties, but he preferred to take an excursion, so long as the drivers had their fair share first. Sometimes he would take Ena and the girls,

but on 29 August they went on their own, because he was not feeling too good. I was in the Sudbury office all day, and he looked in at lunch time; he said he thought he would go home and put his feet up. Later on I went up to Acton and found he had gone to bed. I got him a drink, and he said he felt better, but he would be glad when Ena got home from Walton-on-Naze, which would be about half past eight. I went home to 'Redstacks', but drove to Acton again during the early evening, and found that Billy Bird and his wife had taken charge until Ena got home.

Later the phone rang to say that the doctor had been and had ordered an ambulance to take Bert to hospital in Bury. I sent word to him that he could leave everything in my hands. At about ten the phone rang again, and it was Billy. "The guv'ner", he said, "He's gone. He died as we got him into the ambulance. He'd just lifted his arm to look at his watch"....

LIST OF FULL AND PART-TIME STAFF, WITH EFFECT AS AT 1ST AUGUST 1958

DRIVERS, FULL-TIME

E. Ambrose, Barrow Hill, Acton	SALOONS ONLY	
W. Bird, Old Post Office Row, Acton.	SALOONS ONLY	
R. Charters, Assington	SALOONS ONLY	Has autocycle
G. Edwards, Barrow Hill, Acton	SALOONS ONLY	Has car
W. J. Eley, 46 School Field, Glemsford	ALL TYPES	
C. H. Gibbons, Pool Street, Cavendish	ALL TYPES	Has car
C. Gilson, Bride Street, Barnsbury	SALOONS ONLY	
D. C. Harvey, 2 Bures Rd., Gt.Comard	ALL TYPES	Has car
J. W. Mizon. 47 School Field, Glemsford	ALL TYPES	
L. Parmenter, Queensway, Acton	ALL TYPES	
H. Pleasants, Monks Eleigh	SALOONS ONLY	Has car
K. Plumb, Glemsford	SALOONS ONLY	Has motor cycle
H. Sandford, Acton Place	SALOONS ONLY	
W. Swindells, Barrow Hill, Acton	SALOONS ONLY	

DRIVERS, PART-TIME

R. Chart, The George & Dragon, Melford	ALL TYPES	Has car
W. Ford, Cross Street, Sudbury	ALL TYPES	
P. Sandford, Lofts Fann, Cockfield	SALOONS ONLY	Has car
T. Skinner, Calais Street, Boxford	SALOONS ONLY	

CONDUCTORS. FULL-TIME

A. L. Holt, 26 Hunts Hill, Glemsford	Has driver's licence also
T. Tobin, Sudbury Road, Acton	

CONDUCTORS. PART-TIME

Mrs. J. Ambrose, Barrow Hill, Acton
Mrs. S. Bird, Old Post Office Row, Acton
H. W. Brewster, 1 The Row, Boxted
G. R. Cadge, 11 Cordell Place, Long Melford
A. H. Young, 87 Cordell Place, Long Melford

Chapter Six

RUNNING DOWN

I must have been impossible to live with for the next twelve months. My private life was troubled for much of the time, but that is another story. Nevertheless, it was a very lonely period, despite all of the practical help I received. If I name names it is not in any order of priority, because help came in so many different ways. But it would be wrong not to record – in many cases now too late – the gratitude that I felt then, and feel now.

We try to carry on

All the drivers rallied round, and I cannot recall any industrial problems (as they were in those days politely called) during my year of sole management. This was as true of the men who had joined us from Eddie Long's business as it was from the Corona men. From my days with Premier Travel, through the Corona days, and indeed among my students today, I have come to know an extremely large sample of busmen and women, including a good few who worked for competing firms. Obviously there have been some bad eggs amongst them, but in general I have found them to be among the best friends and the most loyal colleagues I have ever known. And I stress the word colleague, since it was my experience as a manager that we were all facing the same way. Someone had to give the orders, and that was me; someone had to deal with problems, and that was me too; but on the few occasions when we had a bad egg among us he seemed to find some excuse to leave (and no-one criticised if the daily orders gave him a bit of the rougher end). And of course, someone had to take the risk, and that was me, too.

Len Hazell took some of the weight off my shoulders. With the agreement of Eric and Eddie I went on paying Bert's salary to Ena, but she agreed to move with the girls to the Sudbury premises, so that Len and his family could live at Acton. He and I then took alternate days getting the buses out in the morning, and he was also on hand to see that they all came in at night, which had been Bert's responsibility. Someone has to count them all out and count them all in again. Bunkie Chisnell was a tower of strength in the workshops, functioning as chief engineer, and teaching me what little mechanical engineering I came to know; without him we could not have kept the vehicles on the road. Len Hazell took over for a fortnight, subject to my leaving outline daily orders for each day, so that my wife and I could get away later in the summer for a break. (I rang up each night to see how things were going). We stayed with friends and relatives on the south coast, and then worked westward, calling at Emsworth on the way to see Basil Williams, who told us the story of the troubles he had been through in 1952. Finally we had a few days at Ventnor, where I had a dreadful migraine. The whole trip was done by public transport.

My fellow directors showed confidence in me. When we had a board meeting later that year I was presented with the minutes of a previous meeting to sign, which I did not recognise, they recorded that J. Hibbs had been appointed Company

Secretary and those present included him, E. F. Long and E. N. Osborne. To my knowledge one of them was in Scotland and the other in Italy at the time of the supposed meeting, but the accountant told us that the Companies Act required such a meeting to be held immediately upon the death of the previous Secretary, so would I please sign. I was then appointed Managing Director in my own right, and more or less told to get on with it. Eric gave help and advice, but increasingly I came to realise what a good friend I had found in Eddie Long, of whose loyalty and understanding I can never speak too highly. Another bit of welcome help came from the brothers Roger and Anthony Coleby, whom I had known from my Premier Travel days, and who came over on Bank Holidays to help supervise the up loadings, now that I no longer had Bert to keep an eye on the road.

Bert's funeral at the parish church at Acton was attended by all the local bus operators, and several of them went out of the way to speak to me; Jack Mulley among them. Despite our competitive relationship I think they had all wished us well from the start; it has been my experience of business that no-one likes to see another business fail. However much you may stand to gain, there is a real fear of *hubris* and a feeling that it could easily have been you. This was the big, if unspoken, difference between the condolences of the people from Eastern National and Eastern Counties, and the handshake with few words of men like Newton Rule and Barney Jennings, to say nothing of our good friends the Beestons. It is a part of what makes small businesses so much nicer than large ones. I do not want in any way to question the sincerity of men whose personal friendship I came also to value, but empathy and sympathy are two different things, and I prefer the former.

The local CID man came round, as Coroner's Officer, and we had a long talk in my office in Sudbury. He had his job to do, making sure there were no financial complications, and he was polite and, when he saw that all was aboveboard, friendly. For me, though, it was a traumatic interview; I was alone, now, and responsible.

I decided my first priority must be to integrate Long's services and to get the Blackwell licence transferred; the latter depending on the grant of the modified service. I was therefore fully immersed in the detailed side of the business, trying at the same time to oversee the engineering and to control purchasing, and to supervise the accounting. (The last was an immediate problem – why do so many firms submit statements that the layman cannot understand? The fuel bills were the worst). Weekly tickets had been ordered before the takeover and I now introduced them on the former Corona services where timings allowed. The linked operation that had got us into Bury St Edunds became Service 4, but I decided to abandon Bert's policy and to outstation the coach at Eddie's depot at Glemsford, scheduling it into Bury on service from Clare to give a workmen's facility there.

We had now got 19 vehicles, three of them double-deckers. The rest were coaches, except for CLA 103, which was

had a factory on the main road at Glemsford and they asked for a workmen's service. I thought it better to get their people travelling on our local service that passed the works, rather than to tie up vehicles on special workings in the peak. Most existing timing were adequate, but an extra journey was needed from Clare in the mornings, so I decided to run this through to Sudbury, and to extend it to the station to connect with the 8.25 am train. Eastern Counties immediately objected, despite having virtually no *locus.*

Discreet enquiries of Mr Postle, our worthy Stationmaster, informed me that this was at the request of Liverpool Street (who presumably did not *want* any of the additional traffic I was offering them). No doubt I could have succeeded in making them look foolish before the Traffic Commissioners, but it would have been expensive and time-consuming, so I had a further word with Mr Postle and he spoke to someone up the line and the objection was withdrawn. But I still had to get permission to use the station forecourt. After that I used to go to the factory every Friday with a ticket machine, and issue weekly tickets, which were passed to staff at a discount; I returned to the office with the cheque.

At about the same time I put my financial interest before my principles for the second time. Mr Amos, of Belchamp St Paul, had a local service three times a week into Sudbury, and also a workmen's service that was restricted to the employees of CAV. This he applied to open to the public, a useful and sensible idea. But it involved stages at Clare and Cavendish, and this I was not prepared to tolerate. My objection was accepted, and the people of Belchamp and Foxearth never had the service they deserved.

Meantime I worked on the Blackwell application. There was no problem in getting public support from Lavenham and Sudbury for the longer day return or in Cornard for a direct service, but when it came to Bures it was a different matter. Prompted, I was told, by the local mill-owner, the Parish Council informed me that they were not prepared to support the application, and perhaps as a result not one witness would come forward. The reason given was that a direct coach service to London might lead to the closure of the railway station! On 21 November we went to the Traffic Court, and while the early journey from Lavenham was granted along with most of the rest of the timetable, the stages at Bures and Mount Bures were struck out. Thus, I thought, did the middle classes deprive those who could ill afford to go by train of a useful service by road - and I wondered bitterly how many of the middle class actually drove to Marks Tey when they wanted a train to London.

By an ironical twist of fate I was called in as a consultant in 1969 to advise on the fate of what was by then the Sudbury

unmistakably a bus and was commonly known as Clara. There were now seven 29-seat Bedford coaches, but we were still short of luxury vehicles. For this fleet there were 14 full-time drivers and four part-time; two full-time conductors and one part-time (not counting me); an engineer, a greaser and a trainee fitter. In the office there were Len Hazell and Maude Swindells (and me, of course). Only one of the full-time men originally at Acton had 'all types' PSV driving licences, so we had to arrange for tests on a double-decker (which not all of them were keen to take).

With Bunkie's guidance I began to find my feet on the engineering side and to try and get a grip on purchasing, which could easily have got out of hand. Bert had spent a good deal of his time around the running sheds and the workshop at Acton while most of my work had kept me at Sudbury. I was rather pleased though to find a disused airfield near Bury where I could buy ex-military engines for the Bedford *Vistas* for £7.10.0 apiece (£7.50). I bought several, so as to have them in store; it is often quicker to fit a new engine than to tinker about and keep the vehicle off the road. I got some driving experience too, taking every opportunity to handle vehicles running empty, with a view to getting my PSV licence; which, alas, I never achieved.

All this took much longer than it should have done because I had so many calls on my time. At Eric's advice I asked for a postponement of the Blackwell takeover hearing which had been scheduled for 17 September; there was no way I could have had my case prepared in time, and I needed that holiday. Most of the changes to the Long's services were minor, but it was well into the winter before they were all through, including the extension of the Ipswich service to start at Glemsford and the provision of new links from Thurston End to Clare and from Stansfield to Sudbury. It was 27 January 1959 before the Ipswich extension could be introduced, with the terminal there moved from the 'Half Moon & Star' to the Grey Green depot in Old Foundry Road. The rest of the revisions came into effect in the week beginning 23 March, by which time financial problems meant that a printed timetable was beyond our means and everything had to be duplicated.

An example of the problems of licensing was an attempt I made at road-rail coordination. The Barnet Comb Company branch. I argued that it should be kept open to encourage the development of the overspill scheme for Sudbury, and my arguments must have carried some weight, for the line remains open today, with an unmanned halt at Bures.

The storm breaks

By this time, though, I had other problems pressing on me. As the winter set in Len Hazell and I became increasingly aware that revenue was not keeping up to the budget that Bert had prepared. The Glemsford services did as well as expected, but the extra mileage on the former Rippingale and Corona routes was starting to look very dodgy. Far worse, though, was the virtual collapse of the midweek traffic on the London service, while the Bury St Edmunds extension was useless.

At an emergency board meeting I put forward plans to cut mileage, and with the agreement of Eric and Eddie the necessary licence amendments were applied for in November. Though they were fairly minor it was to be March 1959 before they could be introduced; such was the delay involved in the licensing procedure. The main purpose was to cut out 'thin ends'; four days a week the 6 pm from London was to run only to the destination of the last passenger on the coach at Acton, with the late journey out of Stowmarket removed; the 11.15 pm on Saturdays and the 8.15 pm on Sundays were also to turn short when empty. This may not have amounted to a lot, but it would have saved quite a bit of overtime.

That autumn there was a further wage award under the national agreement, and Eric and Eddie agreed that we should pay a similar increase to our staff. They advised against an immediate increase in fares which would have been ill-timed so soon after taking over Eddie's services and would have worsened still more the disastrous fall in traffic already taking place.

We ran into other problems, too. There were several minor accidents, in which no-one was hurt but vehicles were off the road for repair. There was a lot of illness about that winter - "Asian 'flu", they called it. The weather was bad, with ice and snow as the winter deepened, and Skates Hill at Glemsford could be very difficult in such conditions. I seemed to be spending more and more time trying to get vehicles approved by our Vehicle Examiner, who stuck rigidly by the rule-book, while I was trying to save jobs and serve the public. At least his superior, the Certifying Officer, was understanding and helped me greatly in coming to terms with the engineering side of the business.

All the time the strain was building up. I was sleeping badly, and although I tried to get my private life in better order, with more social activity, I am afraid I was the spectre at the feast at some of the parties we gave. Though she tried, my wife proved unable to take any of the burden of the office from me, and in any case she was increasingly involved in the two orchestras she played in, one of which rehearsed at Saffron Walden on Sunday evenings. At Christmas I broke; too tired to eat dinner with the family I spent the day in a sort of coma, trying to keep warm in front of a roaring fire in the sitting room. We never turned a wheel on Christmas day, so I suppose it was the relaxation of tension. Next day I was back in harness, but now the asthma was gripping me.

Only those who suffer from it can really comprehend what it is like to fight for breath when all you want to do is to stop fighting and lie down and rest. It was worst at night, so that I had little sleep, and the loneliness of the struggle seemed almost worse than the fight itself. Much later I was to learn the techniques of relaxation and the ability 'to not fight' which can enable the asthma to be overcome, but fighting it just reinforced its hold over me.

The doctor gave me medicine and told me to take a rest! I explained that I had to see the business through a difficult period and could not afford to get away from it, so he prescribed Cortisone. It was wonderful; suddenly I was free to breathe and I walked as if there was six inches of air beneath my feet. I was over the worst, and better able to cope with each new day, but left with a fear of being alone which took years to exorcise.

There were some good times though, that winter. Ron Chart, landlord of the 'Green Dragon' at Melford, had a PSV drivers licence and used to do some work for us; a good example of the use of part time labour, he would take a coach home and keep it overnight in his yard, and then cover a works contract and a school run. After filling up and sweeping out he got home for the midday opening hours, and then covered the two trips in reverse order. Then the coach was free for the weekend, and none of the regular men ever questioned the procedure. We got the pub outing and the darts club too. And one evening we had a memorable evening at the 'Dragon' when we challenged Premier Travel to a darts match, with a subsequent return fixture at Haverhill. (I date my preference for Greene King's 'Draught Abbot' above all other beers to those days).

The months after Christmas were always the worst financial period of all, and this year the London service took a deep dive. I took what seemed desperate action, driving to Norwich to see the Area Manager of Power Petroleum, our supplier of fuel and (the finance house apart) our largest creditor. He was more than helpful, arranging an immediate moratorium on our outstanding account in return for future payments 'load over load'; i.e. with no new credit. All he asked was to let him know at once if any other creditor put a writ in, so that he did not lose his position. I drove home, relieved, yet depressed because this was so clearly a step down hill. At the bottom of that hill lay liquidation, though I was not admitting it to myself at the time.

The friendship of the staff helped me a lot. Bill and Maude Swindells took a great interest in our children, and lent me records. Bill was a musician and constructed a 'bush bass' out of a tea chest and a broomstick, and we talked about forming a skiffle group. When he took a party for the Suffolk Archaeological Society to the medieval cyder press at Aspal he brought me back a bottle of the stuff, which sold in those days for 2/6 (twelve and a half pence) a quart. I went back for some more.

About this time I applied for a minor development that appealed to me against my study of costing. Each Thursday afternoon we needed a relief from Bulmer Tye into Sudbury, and a similar journey back, later on. My WEA lectures had taken me to Great Henny, which had never had a bus service. So despite the steep hills and narrow lanes I arranged for the Bulmer relief to start at Clay Hills, giving Henny people two hours in Sudbury on market day. It was appreciated, and always found half a dozen passengers, and considering that it cost nothing extra in wages it was well worth while. So that made two villages that Corona had given a bus service fore the first time. Another similar development was to divert the morning service into Stowmarket so as to serve the factories at the south end of the town, this time at the suggestion of our drivers.

I was busy too with a project that Bert and I had put in hand. A firm called United Services Handbooks, which I knew had produced a handsome timetable booklet for Bere Regis and District, contracted to do the same for us. They were to finance it from advertising that they would themselves obtain, and all we had to do was to provide the copy and introduce their representatives to our booking agents. I had once tried my hand at selling advertising in bus timetables for a firm called Guiness and Rawson, and found it very hard to do, but these chaps seemed to have no problems, despite East Anglia being regarded as the salesman's graveyard. As to the contents, I decided to include all the local operators, together with a description of the area and a sales piece about our excursions; though it took a bit of negotiating before I could persuade certain of our neighbours to allow us to include the times of their buses! Eventually, and almost too late, an excellent brochure appeared which we were to sell for sixpence (two and a half pence) a copy. Though it cost us nothing, the publishers suggested we would get rid of more if we made a charge.

This sort of thing helped me keep my confidence. But it was clear by February that our financial situation was serious, and I arranged with Eric to hold a meeting at the accountants' office in London. This was on 18 February 1959, at a time when revenue was always at its lowest ebb. The accountants advised us that we were technically insolvent, and wrote to me a fortnight later, warning us how careful we should be to avoid breaking company law as a consequence of our unanimous decision to continue to trade, at least until the end of the summer. We should try to get the harvest in, we said.

The only way to make significant savings quickly was to withdraw the loss-making journeys from the London service. This meant the 9 am from Kings Cross from Mondays to Fridays with the corresponding up journey at 4.45 pm (though I kept this in from Lavenham on Fridays to work the 9 am down on Saturday mornings. I kept a local on at noon from Sudbury to Lavenham, extended to Bildeston on Thursdays. All of these cuts I wanted to introduce immediately, but to apply them to the period 1 November to 31 May, The 11.15 pm out of London on Saturdays I decided to abandon altogether, since its function was to work a relief coach back in traffic, and we no longer needed a relief through to London on Saturday afternoons. I also provided for the Hadleigh and Bury spurs to be cut along the same lines as the main route.

When I had worked all this out I obtained an interview with Mr Ormond, the Chairman of the Traffic Commissioners, and put the figures before him, with those for the previous year, and my proposals. He fully understood the emergency, but when I asked if he would give me immediate dispensation, he said that he could only do it if I could give him written confirmation form all the local authorities affected that they would not object. That meant two boroughs, four urban districts and at least three rural districts - county councils took little interest in bus services in those days. I went first to Stowmarket and Bury as well as our own two councils at Sudbury. The latter were sympathetic, but in most cases I was told that the matter would have to go to full council, and that there would be no meeting in time to get a decision before the summer season commenced (when I would want to run most of the journeys anyway). So I lodged the applications, intending them to apply from the end of the summer, and we went on losing money.

Assuming still that we would survive, once the summer traffic improved our cash flow, I continued to plan forward. The Gainsborough Tours leaflet for the new season was printed, and I lodged applications to expand the excursion licences that had come with Eddie's business and to add picking up points to the main Sudbury licence for the higher price tours at Glemsford, Cavendish and Clare. On the other side I worked away on the cuts that now seemed inescapable on the local services, and got as far as to lodge applications for the ex-Rippingale routes. I planned also to cut the purely local journeys on the Stowmarket road (the 'doddle') substantially and to reduce the Clare - Bury St Edmunds service to three days a week. In all these areas the expansion we had undertaken had gone sour on us, but I had better luck in fighting off lower

tenders for our school contracts which had been put in by Eastern Counties (despite the dead mileage they would have incurred from their nearest depot at Bury St Edmunds). Work for the Education Committee is like the farmer's milk cheque; income to be relied on in an uncertain world. But those contracts were inter-worked with our local services between Clare and Sudbury, and I think the council officers realised that those services would be at risk.

Keeping quiet about our problems added to the burden, though, and the doctor's treatment only helped my symptoms. Deep down I was weary and depressed. Easter came and went, with the heaviest traffic of the year, and even Bury St Edmunds took a turn for the better, but after Easter came the annual period of low income and inter-hiring bills. On the fifth day of May - my birthday - we held another meeting in London, and I had no fight left in me this time. Even so, the accountants leaned hard, and in one way only: liquidate, they said. (I was to learn later that their junior partner had never done a winding up). Eddie felt it best, and Eric was convinced, so I had no alternative. My wife and I got the train from Liverpool Street, and when I began apparently talking to myself she asked me what I was saying.

It was to repeat from memory those wonderful lines that come at the end of Matthew Arnold's poem 'Sohrab and Rustum', which have carried me through more than one crisis. A great tragedy - far greater than my failed hopes - has befallen Sohrab, and Rustum, his father, who has unknowingly killed his son in single combat. The two armies move away and leave them alone, and Arnold ends the poem - I took my pocket book and wrote it down, there in the crowded train:

> But the majestic river floated on,
> Out of the mist and hum of that low land,
> Into the frosty starlight, and there moved,
> Rejoicing, through the hush'd Chorasmian waste,
> Under the solitary moon; - he flow'd
> Right for the polar star, past Orgunje,
> Brimming, and bright, and large; then sands begin
> To hem his watery march, and dam his streams,
> And spit his current; that for many a league
> The shorn and parcell'd Oxus strains along
> Through beds of sand and matted rushy isles -
> Oxus, forgetting the bright speed he had
> In his high mountain-cradle in Pamere,
> A foil'd circuitous wanderer - till at last
> The long'd-for dash of waves is heard, and wide
> His luminous home of waters opens, bright
> And tranquil, from whose floor the new-bathed stars
> Emerge, and shine upon the Aral sea.

In this way, I suppose, I reassured myself that life goes on when all that it is lived for is taken away, and that beauty - and therefore truth - remains to be sought. A few months later I started to write poetry again myself, something I had given up when I became involved with Corona.

Out of the driving seat

Although we had committed ourselves to liquidation, it was to be 'if all else fails'. We still hoped to be able to sell the business as a going concern, and this was to be my first duty. From this time on, though, I was no longer a free agent; Eric Charles, the partner who had looked after our account and who was to be responsible for the liquidation if it came to that, was now in charge, with me as his agent. My first instruction was to avoid all escapable expenditure, even to the extent of running down the fleet, and a manager without the power to spend is not a manager. Eric Charles produced a budget, to which I had to stick, even though it involved me making a loan to the company to cover wages over a sticky period at the end of May. A special board meeting approved this, and it was subsequently repaid.

Oddly enough my health improved, perhaps because I was free of the burden of responsibility. The same could not be said of my confidence, which had been badly shaken by the catastrophe, which is hardly too strong a words for what had happened. I can only quote from a letter I had a little later, from the late John Birch -

> I think that your courage in entering the business has been very poorly rewarded; you were not to anticipate the misfortunes to fall on the operators of rural services or that in place of the steady expansion of our industry there would be a contraction due to the competition of private transport and entertainment. I am so sorry that you ran into this difficulty.

Unfortunately it was not so easy to see things as clearly as that from where I then stood. But there was plenty to keep me busy. The first and most obvious purchaser was Jack Mulley, who we had always known to have had his eye on the London service. For three months he was to remain the enigmatic character he so enjoyed to be, and my first attempt to sell him the business, lock, stock and tax losses too, was unsuccessful. I saw him several times at the end of May, on one occasion going to Felixstowe to meet him at a pub, since he was driving a coach that day, as he so often did. But I could not persuade him that the business offered him a chance to set off tax; I think he was at heart unwilling to take on the local bus service mileage.

By this time money was getting scarce, and word must have got round that the Corona was in trouble. Eric Osborne had resigned from the board after the meeting on 5 May, under pressure I believe from his partners who felt that it would not do for him to be seen to be associated with a failed business. I thereupon took his place, becoming Chairman, Secretary and Managing Director; a trinity that meant very little in terms of power or prestige! Despite the large sum he stood to lose, Eddie stayed by me, and I can never fully express what his friendship mean to me in the last months of the story.

Eric helped, too, and a practical contribution was the suggestion that we should sell KGV, the newest of the vehicles. When Eddie and I agreed, with the approval of Eric Charles, he set things in train and we got a decent price from Sid Everall, of Kirkby & Sons. But it meant losing our best coach just as the summer season was starting, and it made our problems plain for all to see. Quickly, the vultures began to gather.

Early in June we received a writ. I had obliged a representative by taking a couple of loads of fuel from Jet Petroleum, and they were the first to put the knife in, for £416. I was to learn that those to whom we owed most were to be our best friends, in the weeks that followed. But now there was no way out and the only way to stave off the writs that would follow would be to call a meeting of creditors. Eddie and I had to pay out of our own pockets the cost of answering the writ, which for some reason had been entered in the Wakefield County Court in Yorkshire (not that we had to go there), and the meeting was called for 17 June, at 2.30 pm at Sudbury Town Hall, with me in the chair. I think I went there with my feelings anaesthetised.

It was not a pleasant occasion, with many of the smaller creditors baying for my blood, as it were. Four men held them off: Eric Charles, a Mr A Chilman (who I did not know), Eddie Long (of course), and, above all, Alan Phillips of Bates, Wells & Braithwaite, our solicitor, and a man of unquestioned position in the local community. It was due to them that I came out of the meeting with the confidence to carry on, a confidence that never deserted me. But the sunshine in that dusty room and the almost tangible atmosphere are real to me still.

The creditors had been persuaded that they would be best advised to allow us to go on trying to sell the business. The meeting was to stand adjourned until 15 July, with a moratorium on all debts, and -

> A committee to be appointed to assist the Directors in the management of the Company, and in the negotiations for the sale of the Company as a going concern. The said Committee to consist of the following gentlemen:
> Mr A Chinery, the former proprietor
> Mr E F Long, a present Director, and
> Mr A Chilman, of the Wholesale Traders Association, representing Power Petroleum Co.Ltd.

This committee met two days later at my house and appointed me its secretary and representative. After that the whole of the negotiations were entrusted to me (not by any means at my request), and the committee did little more than endorse what I did. The ball was fully back at my feet, and there it was to stay.

The following weeks were taken up with meetings, letter-writing, minute-keeping and all the organisational matters that the situation required. Later Alan Chinery was to say that that he had not realised I could manage things so well, and that he ought to have taken me on to run the business instead of selling it to Bert and me in the first place. There were still the daily orders to produce and the accounts to be supervised and the vehicles to be worried about. The latter was a melancholy task, for no-one likes to run down a fleet, and when one of the *Tigers* burst a tyre as it arrived from London one day the state of affairs had become public. This brought home the clash of duties that fell to me; under the Road Traffic Act I was responsible for the safety of the vehicles, while under company law I was committed to minimum spending, in the interest of the creditors. Eric Charles reckoned that the latter took priority, but I never felt happy about it.

Lombard Banking allowed us a moratorium on the bills of exchange, while Setright Registers refrained from repossessing the hired ticket machines. In one way or another we kept going, while I sent information to potential purchasers and kept the committee and Eric Charles informed as to all my doings. I typed and stencilled a prospectus, giving what I believed to be a fair statement of the business and its prospects, and this went to the following parties (as well as to a firm of solicitors in Norwich, acting, perhaps, for Eastern Counties) -

> Birch Bros. Ltd., London
> Burton Coaches Ltd., Haverhill
> George Ewer & Co. Ltd. (Grey Green), London
> H C Chambers & Son Ltd., Bures
> F Goldsmith (Sicklesmere) Ltd., Bury St Edmunds
> Moore Bros. (Kelvedon) Ltd.
> Mulleys Motorways Ltd., Ixworth
> P & M Coach Line Ltd., Ipswich
> Premier Travel Ltd., Cambridge
> B A Taylor & Sons, Bildeston
> H S Theobald & Son, Long Melford
> Windsorian Motor Coach Services, Ltd., Windsor

Little came of all this; most of the people concerned drew back when they saw our figures. We were averaging 19 pence a mile (roughly eight new pence) by way of operating cost, which was very low by the standards of the bigger firms, and so if we could not pay our way they certainly couldn't. I think the smaller firms just wanted to take the temperature of the water with a view to the pickings they could expect if we finally collapsed. Only Premier Travel made us an offer, and they had been through the mill themselves. I went to Cambridge on 25 June and talked to Arthur Lainson, and on 30 June Mrs Lainson and Frank Matthews came to Sudbury and looked at our books.

They subsequently offered to take over the company with all its debts, for no consideration, and to keep me on as their manager, and for a day or two I thought we were out of the wood. But Eric Osborne would not hear of it, and Eddie was by no means happy. I suppose they expected still to be able to save some part of their investment, though by this time I could see very limited possibilities of that.

Out-voted on the Premier offer I made one last attempt to sell, this time to our state-owned neighbours. On 15 July the adjourned meeting of creditors took place, and stood adjourned once again, this time to 29 July. I had been able to assure the meeting that there was still the possibility of a sale. The following day the General Managers of Eastern Counties and Eastern National, L H Balls and L E Richards, visited my home and showed a very friendly and sympathetic concern. We were asking £12,500 for the business, but on 21 July Mr Balls wrote to say they were not prepared to buy. Two days later we decided to go ahead with the liquidation on a break-up basis.

The creditors' meeting took place as planned on 29 July and passed the necessary resolutions. Several people told me afterwards that the one surprise was to see me emerge from the meeting, not as the failure they all took me to be but as a member of the Committee of Inspection and as Agent for the Liquidator, our own accountant, Eric Charles, while I had the clear support of Alan Phillips, who had agreed to act as Solicitor to the Liquidator. In its dying days Corona was to be my own show still.

Winding up, and after

The worst thing I had to do then was to write to the shareholders, and to tell Ena, Bert's widow. Guarantees were going to be called in now, and I was - and remain - far more worried about the consequences for those who had trusted me with their money (in Ena's case, with her livelihood) than I was with the trade creditors, who had taken the risks that trade involves. I had to resign from my positions in the Passenger Vehicle Operators Association, and in his reply to my letter F A Walker, the National Secretary, sent me a message that represents all that I felt from other bus and coach operators:

> It really is a tragedy, and I would like to express not only my personal regret, but also the regret of other members of the Committee and your colleagues who would I know, want me at the same time to wish you better fortune in the future.

The weather, which had been poor throughout the summer so far, would not have helped us to survive even if we had not received that writ from Jet Petroleum. The liquidator decided the date for shutting down, and instructed me to give notice to all staff and to arrange to surrender all licences, for both vehicles and services. There was a sense of running to the buffer-stops, but I was too busy to be depressed. Then at the beginning of August, when one day I was in the back office at Sudbury, the phone rang. It was Eric Charles, to say that the weather forecast was good and he thought we should carry on for two more weeks, to obtain the maximum gain for the creditors and to give me more time to negotiate what sales I could. Would I please re-engage all staff.

As I came out into the public office to put this order in motion, Billy Bird met me. "CLA won't start, guv'ner - can you help us shove". I grabbed a packet of Senior Service from the shelf on the counter (we had a tobacconist's licence) and lit up. Now I was back on 20 cigarettes a day, and that helped me see things through. (We got CLA to start).

One or two of the men had already got jobs, but most of them stayed by me to the end. I did all I could to see that they had somewhere to go, but their loyalty seems to me still to be the greatest credit to what Bert and I had set out to do in running Corona the way we did. So far as I know, no-one finished up without work, for by now I had found one firm or another to take over all the road service licences, most of them paying some thing for the good will.

And so the final day - Sunday 9 August 1959 - approached, and on the Saturday I typed out my last daily orders. Newton Rule was to take over the original Corona stage routes; Theobald the ones that came with Eddie Long; and the Rippingale routes were to go to Aubrey Letch of Sible Hedingham, who was himself in the course of selling his business to Donal MacGregor. Taylor of Bildeston had agreed to pay something for the Stowmarket-London service, but no-one wanted the Hadleigh or the former Hartest spurs. All this had been notified to the Clerk to the Traffic Commissioners, and the last thing I had done on the Saturday was to put all the road service licences in the post to his office at Cambridge.

THE LAST TRAFFIC NOTICE
(Running the business had to continue in the midst of winding up).

NOTICE TO ROAD STAFF
Revised Terminal Arrangements at Sudbury

With effect from Sunday 12th July 1959, local services will commence to use the new stands on the Market Hill. This will <u>not</u> apply to London Services, Nos. 1, 1A and 4. The following services will commence at Market Hill and call at Old Market Place as they leave the town:-
    Service 11, Sudbury-Lavenham-Bildeston-Stowmarket
    Service 14, Sudbury-Long Melford-Glemsford
    Service 15, Sudbury-Glemsford-Cavendish-Clare
    Service 23, Sudbury-Acton
    The following services will commence from Old Market Place, and call at Market Hill as they leave the town:-
    Service 17, Sudbury-Gestingthorpe-Braintree
    Services 18/19, Sudbury-Gestingthorpe-Sudbury
    Service 20, Sudbury-Gestingthorpe-Halstead
    Service 21, Sudbury-Twinstead-Halstead
    The following services, which pass through Sudbury, will call at both Market Hill and Old Market Place:-
    Service 16, Glemsford-Sudbury-Ipswich
    Service 30, Clare-Glemsford-Sudbury-Hedingham-Clare

STANDING CONDITIONS
1. No vehicle may wait more than 10 minutes on Market Hill
2. No vehicle may stand on the carriageway at Old Market Place for longer than 10 minutes
3. All layover time which cannot be taken on the forecourt at Old Market Place must be taken in the Station Road Car Park
    Your co-operation is requested in informing the public of these arrangements, and in helping to see to it that they work smoothly.
11th July 1950
Managing Director

[All this was made necessary by the decision of the Council to use the bus stands on the centre of Market Hill as car park space]

That Sunday we ran a Hunstanton excursion and one to Clacton. I saw them off from Old Market Place and went home for some breakfast. Then I went back to see the London coach through at 9.50 am, and when I got home again I said to my wife "Well, that's the last time I shall do that". Virtually at that moment the phone rang. Taylor of Bildeston, it was, to say: "I've 'ad a word with the boys about the London service, an' we don't want it".

Now something had to be done, and at once. If I took no action and word got round, anyone could have had the London service for nothing. I had a plain duty under company law to find a buyer - but where to find an operator with two 41-seaters available at short notice in mid-August? The answer was obvious: Jack Mulley.

I rang Jack at home and put it to him. He said he was just going to put a chicken in the oven, but he would come over right away. This he did, and made me an offer there and then, which I accepted. Now Jack and I could work together, but we had to move quickly. I went back to the office and came home with application forms for road service licences and backings. These I filled up for Jack to sign and wrote a covering letter to the Clerks to the Traffic Commissioners at Cambridge and London asking for 'retrospective dispensation' to run the London service from the following day. Having got all that into the post (there was still a Sunday collection) we went for a drink. On the way he pointed to the odd pair of shoes - one black, one brown - that he was wearing. All through the negotiations he'd worn them, he said, to keep his luck in. And indeed I had been backwards and forwards with offers and refusals more than once. Jack, I decided, was a dealer rather than a businessman, and none the worse for that.

THE LAST DAILY ORDERS

STAFF DETAILS - SUNDAY 9th AUGUST

E. ADDISON	CLA 103	Duty 70 until 6.0pm; Duty 71 from 8.40pm	12.45pm Acton
E. AMBROSE	SICK		
W. BIRD	REST DAY		
R. CHARTERS	CCF 462	Duty 67 D/C until 12.30pm; PH at 1.15pm from Wickham St. Paul to Maldon Car 2; 10.55pm Hadleigh	9.00am Hadleigh
G. EDWARDS	REST DAY		
W. ELEY	REST DAY		
C. GIBBONS	MMP 815	Duty 71 D/C until 5.10pm; evening tour; Duty 70 D/C from 8.55pm	12.15pm Acton
C. GILSON	CCF 120	London driver	8.45am K.X.
J. MIZON	CFW 212	Duty 69	12.45pm Glemsford
L. PARMENTER	DJL 52	In London overnight; relief at 9.00am as far as required; PH at 1.15pm from Wickham St. Paul to Maldon Car 1	8.45am K.X.
H. PLEASANTS	GGV 825	Light to Stowmarket for 8.30am to London & 2.0pm return to Acton	7.30am Acton
K. PLUMB	BGV 783	Duty 65 D/C	8.45am Glemsford
H. SANDFORD	GGV 825	Take Jokey off at 5.20pm; through to Stowmarket for 6.30pm to London & return light	5.15pm Acton
W. SWINDELLS	ECF 305	Light to Hadleigh for 4.15pm to London & 8.15pm return	3.30pm Acton
H. BAKER	CCF 596	Clacton excursion from Stansfield &c, Car 1	8.00am Glemsford
W. FORD	OMT 553	Hunstanton excursion	8.30am Acton
T. SKINNER	CCF 120	Passenger to London to bring bus down	7.15pm Acton
T. TOBIN		Conduct London service until 7.30pm	7.30am Acton
W. HARWOOD		Conduct Duty 70 until 6.00pm; then Duty 71 from 8.40pm	1.15pm Glemsford
A. YOUNG		Conduct Duty 69	1.15pm Melford

I would like to thank all staff for their personal loyalty to me and to say how much I regret that we had to break up like this. Wages for the last few days, together with holiday pay &c, will be available at the Sudbury office from midday on Monday and drivers and conductors wishing for personal testimonials from me should put their names down on the sheet which will be on the counter there.

Next morning Jack's coaches cleared the traffic on both the up and down timings. The drivers reported that Grey Green and possibly another operator had coaches waiting near Kings Cross coach station in case no-one showed up, and A F Braybrooke of Mendlesham was said to have had one waiting at Stowmarket. Jack had stepped in none too soon. And he had taken me on, too, to run what was left of Corona and help with the rest of his business too.

APPLICANTS FOR THE CORONA LICENCES

(Names in bold were successful in obtaining transfer of the appropriate licence)

Service 1	London-Stowmarket	**Mulleys Motorways Ltd**
Service 1A	London-Hadleigh	**Mulleys Motorways Ltd**
Service 4	London-Rede	**Mulleys Motorways Ltd**
Service 7	Wattisham RAF Station-London	Partridge & Son (H J Claireaux); Combs Coaches Ltd; **Mulleys Motorways Ltd**
Service 11/22	Sudbury-Stowmarket	Mulleys Motorways Ltd; **N S Rule**
Service 12	Clare-Bury St Edmunds	F Goldsmith (Sicklesmere) Ltd; Nichols (Clare) Ltd; **H S Theobald**
Service 13	Cavendish-Bury St Edmunds	F Goldsmith (Sicklesmere) Ltd; Mulleys Motorways Ltd. **H S Theobald**
Service 15/30	Clare-Sudbury	F Goldsmith (Sicklesmere) Ltd; Nichols (Clare) Ltd; **H S Theobald**
Service 16	Glemsford-Ipswich	F Goldsmith (Sicklesmere) Ltd; Mulleys Motorways Ltd; **N S Rule**
Service 17	Sudbury-Braintree	**A E Letch**
Service 18/19	Sudbury-Gestingthorpe-Sudbury	**A E Letch**
Service 20	Sudbury-Gestingthorpe-Halstead	**A E Letch**
Service 21	Sudbury-Twinstead-Halstead	**A E Letch**
Service 23	Sudbury-Acton-Sudbury	Mulleys Motorways Ltd; **N S Rule**
Service 25	Great Maplestead-Sudbury	**A E Letch**

Excursions originating from:

Sudbury	H C Chambers & Son; F Goldsmith (Sicklesmere) Ltd; **Mulleys Motorways Ltd**; H S Theobald
Long Melford	F Goldsmith (Sicklesmere) Ltd; **Mulleys Motorways Ltd**; H S Theobald
Glemsford	F Goldsmith (Sickleemere) Ltd; **Mulleys Motorways Ltd**; H S Theobald
Fenstead End	F Goldsmith (Sicklesmere) Ltd; B K Jennings; **Mulleys Motorways Ltd**; Nichols (Clare) Ltd
Gestingthorpe	**A E Letch**

BELOW: Sixteen years on, and the town service bus is seen here at Sudbury Bus Station, still showing the Corona fleet name. *(P F Clark)*

Chapter Seven

THE AFTERMATH OF THE STORM

Working for Jack

The next morning Jack was over in Sudbury again, and we walked together in the sunshine down Market Hill and Friars Street to see Alan Phillips and make the offer formal. He wanted, he said, the London service and the Hadleigh and Hartest spurs - no nonsense about Rede - together with the Wattisham RAF service and the excursions that had been licensed originally to Corona and Long. For reasons that escape me now he said he would run the Wednesday and Saturday services from Cavendish and Glemsford to Bury. He also told me that I could expect, shall we say, an honorarium, if my efforts succeeded in getting the licences transferred to him. Since I was now working for him, and no longer for the liquidator, this struck me as eminently reasonable. So far as the property was concerned, he would pay off the mortgage and acquire it in his own name. Apart from this, he said he would pay Syd Blackwell the amount outstanding, though he did not want the Blackwell service, and he was as good as his word, which relieved my conscience considerably. (Syd had already put in an application to cut the service, which had been as hard hit as our own).

During the next few weeks I spent most of my time getting to know more about Jack's business as well as helping Eric Charles with the winding up; while at the same time trying to sort out my personal life. I knew I would have to sell my house, but my wife refused to accept Jack's offer of accommodation at Old Market Place on the grounds that this would mean turning out Ena and the girls (though Jack was ready to find them somewhere to live, and later on they had to move out anyway). The outcome of all that is a different story, but I think my lack of a home made Jack a bit doubtful as to how long I would be around.

So far as the business was concerned, though, I had survived. More, the ball was still at my feet – Alan Chinery was heard to say to someone (the word got back to Jack) "I thought that Hibbs was done for, and now Mulley's employing him to run the business". On 11 September there was a sale at Acton, when 'Vehicle Equipment, Machinery, Spares and Office Equipment' went under the hammer, and people from half the county were there. Before Harry Turner commenced the auction Jack turned to me and asked me to fetch something for him from the Sudbury office - "Take the car, John" he said, in the hearing of everyone, and gave me the keys of his new Jaguar Mark VI. That gesture typifies for me the generous spirit of a man from whom I was to learn a great deal about running a coach business.

Late in October the applications for the transfer of the licences were listed - we had been running on 'short period' authority till then. The principal objectors were British Railways, Eastern Counties and Eastern National for the London services, with various local operators for the excursions. Theobald contested the transfer of the Cavendish-Bury licence, while the remaining transfers had by then all been settled, and the sales I had arranged with Letch, Rule and Theobald had all been honoured. Two days before the furniture was to be removed from my house for storage we went to the Traffic Court at Cambridge once again.

Alan Phillips took the case for us, and he opened by saying that he was there "with fire in his belly". He had Colonel Tuck, the Mayor of Sudbury, as our principal witness, saying how essential the Council considered the London service to be. Mr Ormond, the Chairman of Commissioners, announced that he

BELOW: The Corona livery in Mulleys' ownership - a service coach at Kings Cross. *(P. D. Moth)*

ABOVE: A more upmarket example of Mulleys' Corona livery, on a Duple Britannia bodied AEC Reliance, taken at the Brighton Coach Rally. *(P. D. Moth)*

BELOW: Wartime 'utility' double-deck Guy Arab, BJG 440, new to East Kent Road Car, carrying an odd mixture of information, for a Mulleys bus which never worked any of the services mentioned. *Author's collection.*

had been advised that they were obliged to grant the application if it were shown that a business existed to sell. Eastern Counties, as the lead objector, then concentrated upon trying to show that the service was not worth running, using data they had obtained from their earlier negotiations with me for the sale of the whole business. Bill Hall, their renowned Traffic Manager, said they would not buy it, nor even take it over for nothing. Yet in 1962 Eastern Counties paid Jack a substantial sum for the good will - surely a classic example of the difference between a forced sale and 'a willing buyer and a willing seller'.

At the end of the day the Commissioners granted the London services to Jack and the excursions as well. We could not show that any consideration had been paid for the Cavendish-Bury service, and Theobald had the better case, so we lost that. The Wattisham service could have proved tricky, but we got the third share, giving us the majority interest; but the traffic was already dying. For Jack, now, I think a dream had come true.

This, though, is not a book about Mulleys Motorways. The day-to-day running of the Sudbury business was no longer in my hands; Eileen Nice, Jack's capable manager, and Len Hazell dealt with that. Jack kept the Corona fleet name, but with vehicles in his own colours of cream and orange, and he took the same sort of detailed interest in an apparently detached way that he took in all of his operations. One day he told me that a lady from London had been explaining how much better the service had been when Mr Davidson and Mr Hibbs had it; he recognised my description of her. So I told him how she had

said how much better Mr Chinery had run it, after Bert and I took over. The story pleased him as much as it did me, for Jack had the true Suffolk man's ability to enjoy a joke at his own expense.

Eric Charles meanwhile arranged the sale of the Corona vehicles. They had been standing at Acton since August, but now various dealers began to prowl round them, including men with magnets, checking the amount of non-ferrous metal in those that would go for breaking up. Some of the *Vistas* went to Cyprus, where no doubt they had a long and honourable career. In the end the whole fleet fetched £3,425, while Bert had valued it in 1958 at £6,025. In Appendix 3 enthusiasts will be able to see where some of the vehicles went, but there is a touching story here, concerning CCF 463, the AEC *Regal III* that had been one of our workhorses. She got as far as Halstead and there broke down, finishing in Syd Blackwell's yard, where her radiator shell remained for some years on display. You get attached to machines that have served you well, and I felt grateful to CCF for lasting out to the end.

I did what I could to develop business for Jack. First there was the Sudbury town service. Not having any local services, we had a 29-seater idle at Acton all day when the schools were open, having worked one of the contracts. People had often asked me to put on a bus to take them home to the council estates, some of which involved an uphill walk. I figured out that, since we were paying the driver anyway, we could make such a service pay with a minimum average load of

BELOW: The launch of the Sudbury town service In 1960. Jack Mulley (on the left) talking to Colonel Tuck, the Mayor of Sudbury – the author standing behind him, with ticket machine. Alan Chinery is wearing the dark brown felt hat, and behind him stands Mr Postle, the Station Master. *(Suffolk Free Press)*

four or five passengers, and that after allowing for the loss of the coach on Saturdays and in the school holidays, when there might be other work for it to do. Jack saw the point at once – the idea of escapable cost is built into small business practice in the bus and coach industry, even if the words are not well understood. Despite objection by Eastern Counties we got the licence, and the average load turned out to be ten. Later on I extended a few journeys to the village of Middleton, another place that had never had a bus service, at the suggestion of Mr & Mrs Prince, whose friendship I had come to value – Middleton paid, too.

The service was duly launched by the Mayor at a small ceremony on Market Hill, attended also by Mr & Mrs Chinery, and Arthur Lainson and Frank Matthews from Premier Travel. Jack was extremely pleased with himself, and I think he had high hopes of me. He bought several *Tigers* from Grey Green and a handsome vehicle with the Harrington 'fin' from Scarlet & Blue of Minehead. These, he said, were 'for me'. I am afraid I let him down, though, for subsequent attempts at development were less successful.

First we tried for summer Saturday seaside services. Jack already ran from Bury to Yarmouth, so we applied to start that service from Halstead, picking up at various points by way of Sudbury and Lavenham. At the same time we applied for an entirely new service from Thetford via Bury and Sudbury to Clacton and Walton. I had always had such ideas in mind but could never spare the coaches; yet Jack, even with the London service to run, was never short. The applications were listed with objections from British Railways, Eastern Counties and several independents, but it proved impossible to collect an adequate supply of public witnesses, and Jack lost interest, so both were withdrawn.

At the same time, though, we applied to start the Rede service at Bury St Edmunds. Jack had tried before to get a Bury-London licence but with no success - the licensing system seemed from time to time to throw up a case where it became a matter of prestige to keep an interloper out, making it very hard to obtain a grant. It is fair to say that in some cases the whole system became ensnared by its own procedure, so that the outsider met with what amounted to a stone wall – and Mulleys Motorways was a classic example of the 'outsider'.

The serious objections came once more from British Railways and Eastern Counties. We retained Counsel, and I advised Jack's Solicitor to get a man who had impressed me in Traffic Court cases before, which he did. (Counsel went so far as to suggest that I had lunch with him, much to the Solicitor's disgust, but the Traffic Courts were never bound by standard rules of procedure). We made the best case we could but it was not strong enough, and we lost. The support we got from Bury St Edmunds was nothing like as strong as I would have expected for something similar at Sudbury, so our case did not look as good as I would have wanted it. (I think I have a touch of the Sudbury feelings about Bury, which I know are reciprocated). But to be honest, I doubt whether the traffic would ever have come to much; looking back I am inclined to see Bury St Edmunds as 'fairy gold', which we should have ignored, just as Alan Chinery ignored it in 1929 when he chose Stowmarket for his outer terminal.

Meantime I had decided to look elsewhere for my future, if only to keep my family together, given that my wife did not want me to work for Jack. I had three interviews in the autumn with the British Transport Costing Service, and in December Basil Williams offered me a job, running 'Glider and Blue', which he had just bought. At the end of the year, resulting from the meeting I had had with Mr Balls and Mr Richards, I was interviewed at No. 10 Fleet Street by the Tilling board with Maurice Holmes QC, himself a former Essex independent operator, in the chair. Perhaps it was fate that caused the borrowed car to break down, so that I arrived late and ill-prepared for the interview; anyway, I did not get the job. After Christmas I had a long talk at the *Blue Boar* in Cambridge with A F R Carling of BET, which led to an interview at Stratton House. It was suggested that I might find a niche as a sort of trouble-shooter for the Group, and no doubt I could have made a good career there. But they had their doubts, I could see, and eventually I threw it all away - by giving an honest answer. "Mr Hibbs, what to you *really* want to do?", someone asked. My reply was "I want to write", and I knew at once I had said the wrong thing. British industry distrusts the slightest sign of the 'intellectual'.

Gilbert Ponsonby's confidence in me gave me great strength and support. He gave me a year's subscription to *The Economist* to help with job-hunting, and he suggested I should try and get into teaching. I had an interview with Howard Stebbings at the Institute of Transport, which led to further interviews at City of London College and North West Polytechnic, but nothing came of them. In May I gave oral evidence to the Jack Committee on Rural Bus Services, where I met David St John Thomas, who was later to publish my first hardback book. In the summer my wife took the two boys to Germany, and I lodged in Great Cornard with a friend of ours, and tried to start writing that book, *The History of British Bus Services*. They came back in October and soon after I told Jack that I felt we had come to the parting of the ways. We shook hands on it, and I found myself without a job, and this time without a home either.

I tried for various posts, but at 35 it took time to find a new berth. Jack was as good as his words about the promised

ABOVE: Owned by Combs Coaches, painted in Mulleys livery and with a Corona fleet name, the flag was still flying when this picture was taken in October 1976. *(P. F. Clark)*

honorarium; when I went to see him he said "I never thought you'd ask". I had some lecturing, for the WEA and the London University Extra-Mural Certificate in Transport, and divided my time between my mother's home at Brightlingsea, my wife's parents' home at Cambridge, and various friends. It was a depressing period - "hope deferred maketh the heart sick" - but towards the end of the year I was offered interviews with several organisations. I went hardest for the post in London, on the argument that it is there that a man can best repair his fortunes, and in January 1961 I was appointed Traffic Survey Officer at British Railways' Eastern Region headquarters at Liverpool Street. The dream of buses was very much over, now.

Reflections

Afterwards there were those who said "I told you so" and others who advised me not to set my sights too high. Transport operators in the private sector, where you have to face the risk of failure, without exception continued to show me continued respect, which is one reason why I believe the private sector to be better suited to provide public transport than the 'professionals'. The difficulties in the way of winding up a publicly owned business can only dull the edge of managerial efficiency, while there were many who would have been thinking "there but for the grace of God go I".

But as well as risk there is a great satisfaction in running your own business, and Bert Davidson and I were seeking something more than the financial rewards. Corona worked remarkably well as a team; perhaps I would say as a ship's company. A business such as this is held together by something more than the contractual relationship between employer and employee; it is a community in which mutual respect overrides the formal rules. I still regret as much as anything the loss of so many friends when the story ended. Those who remain to read these pages must know that they are not forgotten.

I have always missed, too, the involvement with the people and the community that comes from running bus services on a small scale. No-one at Norwich or Chelmsford could have the *feel* for the services I had, and this is a serious fault in all large firms. The transport industry can never be properly managed by men and women sitting behind desks, let alone those who are mesmerised by the career structure which can easily become more important than the work they are there to do. In a small firm you know that you are there to do a job, and you can see why; in a large one it is too easy to see the job as being there for *your* sake, rather than you being there for the sake of the job.

Nevertheless we did wind up the business, and on 19 October 1960 the final meeting of creditors took place at the Berners Hotel in London, when a dividend was declared of two shillings and ninepence-halfpenny (app. 14p) in the pound (which was more than had been predicted a year before). A lot of people lost money in our collapse, myself not least. Now it is in the nature of business to take risks, and so, as I have already said, I feel that the trade creditors deserve a word of regret, but no more. After all, those who had most at stake wanted us to weather the storm. The staff received all that was due to them (as required by law), and none of the men finished without work. Those who remain on my conscience are those who backed us, and above all Bert's widow, Ena. The others include my mother; our anonymous backer (known to me and Bert), who had made the venture possible; Alan Chinery, who may have set a high price, but who left a fair amount on credit (he died five years later, aged 70); and most especially Eddie Long, who trusted us and never complained. Could it have been avoided?

Hindsight is dangerous, but I suppose in a way it could. It is true that we were over-stretched on borrowings, but there is a stage in the expansion of a business when turnover may not be increasing fast enough to carry the overhead costs, and in the ordinary way this is where credit is applied in order to promote growth. Together we could have managed a business quite a bit larger with no additional effort, but after Bert's death I needed a traffic manager to take the detail off my hands and leave me free to act as general manager, as I should, yet I could not afford to pay the salary. Nevertheless, it was external forces that started the decline.

By the end we were certainly overtrading, but the unforeseeable sharp fall of traffic in the winter of 1958-1959 came on the London services that were our mainstay just as much as on the local bus services, and the London services carried the heaviest mileage. The turning-point came when the rigidities of the licensing system blocked the decision to cut mileage, and thus perhaps let us turn the corner; though the wet summer of 1959 might have upset my calculations.

Some forty years on, what does it matter? To me, those days remain open in my mind, not tinged by nostalgia, forming a picture marked by a certain kind of reality that comes from doing a recognisably and immediately useful kind of job. I think many desk-bound managers in big companies might envy me that. And I owe a debt of gratitude for it to all who backed me, advised me, and worked with and for me, including always the shade of Bert Davidson. I was the lucky one, the survivor.

Chapter Eight

EPILOGUE:
Is There Something to be Learnt?

Whether Bert and I were right to risk our own and other people's money in such a venture I must leave the reader to decide. We would never have made our fortunes but then we never expected to. Our plan was to capitalise our efforts and to build up a business that we could go on running at an easier pace as we grew older so that, as Bert put it, we would never need to actually retire. Neither of us were 'nine-to-five' men and I think that was the sort of plan that would have had the approval of Adam Smith – or of Friedrich Hayek. So what was to have been our strategy, in seeking to implement the plan?

What follows may not have been clearly articulated in our minds but I believe it represents pretty well how we were thinking and it may illustrate the kind of strategy a bus business needs, even if in our case it was overtaken by events. Otherwise I believe it would have been the foundation for success in realising our plan. I had learned when working with Premier Travel how to schedule buses and crews so as to get the maximum revenue-earning mileage, and I had learned too that the criterion for assessing net revenue is marginal cost, and not the average cost/average revenue equation universally to be found in the bigger firms in the bus industry then, and for many years thereafter. This had been reinforced for me by Ponsonby's teaching at the London School of Economics – I can hear his voice now, saying "any mileage that covers its escapable costs and makes a contribution, however small, to overheads is worth while running".

The big firms in those days were trapped in a downward spiral of averages. Mileage that earned less in revenue per car mile than the company's average cost per car mile tended to be abandoned, with the effect that overheads had to be carried on less mileage, so that the average cost per car mile rose, leading to yet further cuts. It seemed to me mad then, and it does now, but there were many who said I was mad myself to question it. To make matters worse, some of the state-owned

bus companies persuaded the Traffic Commissioners to allow them a higher price per mile on rural services, on the same allocatory principle, thus driving away their most vulnerable traffic as rural car ownership started to spread.

Instead of this, having got the fleet down to what seemed to us to be a minimum size for survival, I made sure, so far as I could, that every bit of net revenue that was going came our way, whatever that might have done to the load factor. Where I could see an opportunity and had a vehicle and driver idle in paid time, I sought to expand into the gaps. There were plenty of them, and I could spot them because I was closely involved and familiar with the countryside we served and fascinated by the challenge of it all.

But that was only one wing of the strategy, and of course we would have rapidly gone out of business if that had been our sole revenue. It is like working out whether you can afford to run a car by taking nothing into account but the cost of petrol. Certainly there were innovations that earned much more than their out-of-pocket cost, such as the addition of commuter journeys between Lavenham and Sudbury, but you cannot set out to exploit the marginal cost principle unless you have a sound core of high-revenue mileage. At the end of the day, average revenue must equal and exceed average cost per vehicle mile. For every mile of marginal net revenue there must be a mile of high income to complement it. The skill of bus management is to successfully walk this constantly changing tightrope, to reach the safe landing of success.

This, though, is not the sort of cross-subsidy that in those days the big companies said they needed the licensing system to provide. That only exists where mileage involves an actual, continued and significant net deficit, to support which there has to be an opportunity to extract a monopoly profit elsewhere. The fact that the big companies' operating costs were higher than the typical small rural operator made even less sense of their argument, but there it was. But the logical corollary of

BELOW: BMR 690, formerly in Rippingale's fleet, stands at Chelmsford on a private hire duty. *(P. J. Snell)*

the costing theory I have tried to explain is the use of a variable pricing structure, based upon 'what the traffic will bear', which in those days was forbidden by the licensing system and is not, I suspect, fully understood today. Anyway, that aspect of strategy was not open to us to explore.

For a business to survive there must thus be a substantial core of mileage that is earning a healthy return above marginal cost. With that you can afford to maximise the contribution of the bits and pieces, like my extensions to serve the Maplesteads and Great Henny and the diversions via Semer and Preston St. Mary, not to mention scheduled dead mileage like the 11.15pm out of London on Saturday nights. And you can look for extra profit in less price-sensitive areas, which for us meant the programme of up-market excursions and the Gainsborough Tours promotion, with its opportunity for a healthy mark-up. Private hire rates were always under competitive pressure, though we had loyal customers who were prepared to pay more for the vehicles and drivers we employed.

So what went wrong with the strategy? Just that the revenue from the core mileage collapsed, suddenly and unexpectedly, in that winter of 1958-1959. Without it the contributory mileage became a liability, while at the same time the 'jam' was spread more thinly, on account of the two wet summers. The alternative smaller core in the form of Eddie Long's mileage was not big enough to balance the strategy, while the Bury St. Edmunds extension, our one big mistake, was pretty certainly in permanent net deficit. If there is a lesson here it is that a business will be at risk so long as it is small enough to depend upon one main source of viable revenue.

I think the lesson I would draw is the vulnerability of a business like ours when seeking to expand. Just what it was that hit the London traffic we never knew, though the period was one of economic uncertainty and the cost of living, based on the index of retail prices with 1948 as 100, rose to 140.4 in 1956, 145.7 in 1957 and 150.1 in 1958 (after which the rate of increase eased off for a year or two). What should be remembered is that the crisis was hardly to have been foreseen, so that a prompt response was essential for survival. That prompt response was denied us by the licensing system.

Is it possible that we might yet have survived. The confidence shown by Premier Travel in their offer to acquire the business with its debts suggests it. The road service licences, after all, represented valuable monopoly assets. And I have no doubt that, had Bert still have been alive, we could have found a way round our troubles, for the most serious problem, as I look back, was my continued involvement with the day-to-day running of the business in all its aspects.

It was doubtless the tension generated by this conflict that led to my stress related illness, which weakened my self-confidence at the time when I ought to have been resisting the pressure from our accountants to go for a forced sale. Eddie and I might have made a bid for the core business – the Clare road and London – while disposing of the village services in the way they eventually went. In such a scenario Blackwell's residual traffic would have been worth having, and while marginal for a time, London services generally recovered a few years later. If Premier had taken the business over I think their strategy would have been the same.

On the other hand, I sometimes wonder how big we could have grown before either diminishing returns set in or it ceased to be fun to manage the business. I think it would have turned upon the stage at which we ceased to be a coach operator running services. In the coaching trade you have to keep in close touch with your customers, whereas in a medium to large bus company the individual passenger does not count for much. I am sure the number of staff comes into it too, for I had learned when with Premier Travel how important it is to know the men and women on the road, and that would have been at risk when we were no longer on the road ourselves. A. T. James, of BET, was the last of the older generation then in the business who had been a conductor and when I appeared before the Jack Committee, of which he was a member, I was able to appeal to his experience still.

It was sad to watch the way in which management at a distance messed up the London service and fascinating to see how later it reverted to its original route from Stowmarket, on pretty well the times we worked to. If I have any overall conclusion, it must be that bus companies should not get too large for personal management (coach companies cannot afford to), and managers need something of the enthusiast in their makeup to gain a personal satisfaction from success in serving their community, at a profit.

INDEPENDENT BUS SERVICES IN SOUTH-WEST SUFFOLK

Conclusion of a paper presented by the author at a meeting of the Omnibus Society in London on 27 February 1953. Reproduced by permission of the Society.

I am going to throw out some suggestions, and I hope that you will take them up and tell me I am wrong if you feel so disposed. But the future of the omnibus industry is not, as we are perhaps still inclined to think, an assured one; and I am sure we have something to learn from the smaller operator. A repeated increase in the tax on fuel has led to a series of fare increases, which, as a matter of interest, commenced with the Eastern Counties company. Now, when these fares increases have been applied for, some startling things have been said about the finances of great operating concerns, and much has been set out in illustration of the increased costs of operation, yet, I would have you notice, the small operator time and time again has had to be almost dragged along against his will and judgement. Could it be that the small man has the lower costs? I am sure he has, and - here is something positive - I suggest that many of the non-paying routes of the large concerns might well be sold to other operators who could make a living from them.

Perhaps I had better leave that suggestion where it stands, though I hope you will not be content to do so, and be for a moment perhaps a little less controversial. It is I believe a fact that in many parts of the country the smaller operators have a better 'name' with the public than the larger. There are of course exceptions both ways, but I submit that it is a general rule. Let us see if we can find the reasons for this. We are told that large size makes for economies of scale, but I suggest that it also makes for certain diseconomies of scale, and that the transport industry is particularly liable to these.

ABOVE: A *Primrose* Leyland SKP, new in 1935, working one of the other Essex coach services. This was Chelmsford-London, but it was withdrawn before we could make an offer for it. *(Essex Bus Enthusiasts Group)*

complicated subject of car-workings. The small operator however can often lay out his half-dozen services on a permanent scheme of car-working, and leave it all unchanged for twenty years, while he sits back and concentrates on his maintenance and private hire bookings. And thus is reliability achieved, for however much a change is advertised, always there will be someone who has not heard of it, and who will write to complain (or not even write) that the 'bus did not turn up' - and one such grievance can lose a great deal of good will.

One of the great economies of scale is said to be the use of centralised purchasing of supplies, spare parts etc. This is perfectly within the reach of small-scale operators working together in co-operatives. Similarly maintenance can be reduced in cost if a number of operators enter into a common agreement for periodical overhauls by a commercial firm, which could thus benefit by a steady supply of work In sheer efficiency of management I do not believe that scale plays any

significant part; it depends very much upon the man at the top in either case, and a man running his own small business may do so just as well as the head of a large public company. It is for each to make the most of the advantages of his own type of operation, and it must not be forgotten that one man may be fitted to handle a small firm who would be quite unsuited for the management of a large concern, and vice versa.

For my own part, I incline to the view that, with certain exceptions, the small man is best suited to the operation of local services, as opposed to inter-urban services, for which the large undertaking is perhaps better fitted. And indeed when one looks at the origin of bus services in country districts, one

Public relations, for instance, are definitely more expensive when they mean the employment of highly paid officers to deal with them than when they merely involve meeting the passengers casually in the local, and I am not at all sure that they are necessarily less efficient. Again, in rural areas the public prefers its timetables to remain unchanged over a period of years, and many of the operators whom we have been discussing print no timetables at all, because it is literally a case of 'everyone knows when the bus goes'. But a large firm may have to alter timetables quite frequently, for perfectly sound reasons, and often the necessary modification of one service leads to consequent and rather arbitrary changes in several others, owing to that very

ABOVE: Amos, of Blechamp St Paul, bought this Bedford/Duple OWB, with a 32-seat 'utility' body, new in 1944, to keep his rural services running. Here it is on Sudbury Market Hill, probably on a Saturday, waiting to return home. 'Billy' Amos died at the end of 2002, at the age of 80. *(Essex Bus Enthusiasts Group)*

BELOW: Chambers' Guy Arab IV, new in 1957, stands on Angel Hill, Bury St Edmunds, ready for the long run through to Colchester. We all respected the smart turnout of Chambers' fleet. *(P. F. Clark)*

ABOVE: Jennings of Ashen owned two Leyland Olympics, both originally demonstrators, which were mainly used on his Clare-London service; this HR44, seen at Braintree on market day, gave us the idea for a dual-purpose bus, which in our case was an AEC/Burlingham Reliance. *(P. F. Clark)*

often finds the small firm developing from the country carrier, while the large firm was started perhaps by national interests (with or without the capital N) sending down from London a few men and machines to commence operation over the main roads around some provincial town. But I would have no cast-iron rule as to who should run where; there must always be exceptions to this kind of thing.

Now I will not keep you waiting much longer, for I look forward to discussing these points, and any others you may care to raise. Just one final word - I do deplore, and ask you to consider, the present ring-fence round the industry as far as bus services are concerned, so that under the Road Traffic Act as it stands at present we can only look forward to the eventual disappearance of the small-scale operator, with all his advantages or disadvantages, owing to a legal barrier that stops anyone new from getting in.

LEFT: A Leyland PD2/10, originally owned by St Helens Corporation, but later operated by Theobald on the former Corona Sudbury–Glemsford service. *(P F Clark)*

FLEET LISTS

The data in these fleet lists has been compiled from various sources, including the PSV Circle. Additional information or corrections will be welcome, and should be addressed to the author, **c/o the publishers**

LIST 1 - A A CHINERY, LATER CORONA COACHES LTD

Livery: Chocolate and tangerine
Asterisk identifies fleet at closure

Fleet no.	Regn. number	Chassis type/ builder	Body &c	Seating	History
	CF 8140	? Chevrolet	?	?16?	New 1/28. Burnt out ? date
	CF 0166	Gilford	United	C32?	New 4/29. Sold to ?, ? date
	CF 9414	Chevrolet	?	? ? ?	New 8/29. Burnt out ? date
	GV 411	Leyland TS1	Petty	C ? ?	New 6/31. To Argosy, London, ? Date
	GV 819	Bedford WLB	Duple	B20F	New 10/31. To Darlington, Potter Street 6/39
16	GV 883	Leyland KP2	Duple	C24?	New 11/31. To R H Jones, Rhostryfan 3/38
18	GV 1061	AEC Regal	Petty	C32C	New 3/32. To Doran, Thetford 7/38
17	GV 1062	Morris Director	Duple	C20?	New 5/32. To Burgoin, Haverhill 7/37
19	GV 1655	AEC Regal	Duple	C32?	New 4/33. To Ashdown, Danbury 1/41
	GV 2604	Dodge KB	? Duple	C20F	New 7/34. To Reeve, Reepham 10/37
	GV 2605	Leyland KP3	Duple	C24F	New 7/34. To Burgoin, Haverhill 1/41
	GV 3289	AEC Q	Duple	C32?	New 4/35. To Cooper, Combs 5/38
	GV 3423	Leyland KP3	Duple	C24?	New 6/35. To Ashdown, Danbury 1/41
	GV 5771	Bedford WTB	Duple	C20F	New 11/37. To PW Balls, Newmarket 11/54 (Mobile shop)
	GV 6035	Leyland KPZ2	Duple	C25F	New 2/38. To Shanks, Hunstanton 10/53
	GV 6065	Leyland TS8	Duple	C32F	New 3/38. To Ansell, London 10/49
	GV 6066	Leyland TS8	Duple	C32F	New 3/38. To Ansell, London 10/49
	GV 6209	Bedford WTB	Duple	C25F	New 5/38. To Stewart, Bury St Edmunds 10/49
	GV 7168	Leyland KPZ2	Duple	C26F	New 7/39. Sold to ?, 1953
	GV 9494	Bedford OWB	Duple	B32F	New 12/45. To Banwell, Newport 3/50
	AGV 696	Leyland PS1/1	Strachan	C32F	New 8/47. To Hardy, Darlington 2/51
	AGV 772	AEC Regal III	Gurney Nutting	C33F	New 12/47. To Ruby, Leicester 3/52
38	BGV 782*	Bedford OB	Duple	C29F	New 7/49. Sold for export (Cyprus) 9/59
39	BGV 783*	Bedford OB	Lucas	C29F	New 8/49. To Sleeman, London 9/59
41	CCF 462*	Bedford OB	Thurgood	C29F	New 12/49. To Bayhead, Ascot 9/59
42	CCF 463*	AEC Regal III	Windover	C33F	New 12/49. To Blackwell, Earls Colne 9/59 (broken up)
45	CCF 595*	Leyland PS1/1	Gurney Nutting	C35F	New 5/50. To Shaw, Maxey 9/59
46	CCF 596*	Leyland PS1/1	Gurney Nutting	C35F	New 5/50 To Shaw, Maxey 9/59
	DGV 123	Bedford SB	Duple	C33F	New 8/51. To Hull, Great Barford 11/57
47	ECF 305*	AEC Regal IV	Gurney Nutting	C41C	New 3/52. To Warren, Ticehurst 9/59
	FGV 174	Bedford SB	Duple	C37F	New 9/53. To Jones, Pitt 2/57
44	OMT 553*	Bedford OB	Duple	C29F	From JM, London, 12/54 To Sleeman, London 9/59
48	GGV 823*	Bedford SBG	Duple	C38F	New 1/55. To Hertfordian, Harrow 9/59
	BMR 690	Bedford WTB	Willmott	C20F	From Rippingale 5/56 To Tivey (?) 3/57
	GV 5837	Bedford WTB	Duple	C26F	From Rippingale 5/56 Sold to ?, 2/57
49	KGV 195	AEC Reliance	Burlingham	DP41F	New 6/57. To Howell & Withers, Pontllanfraith 6/59
30	BTW 374*	Leyland LT5A	Wilks & Meade	C35F	From Long, 8/58 To Price, Basildon 9/59
31	CLA 103*	Leyland LT7	ECW	B35R	From Long 8/58 Sold 9/59 (to showman)
32	GHU 489*	Bristol K5G	Bristol	H30/26R	From Long 8/58. To Price, Basildon 9/59
33	DSG 168	AEC Regent	Brush	L27/26R	From Long 8/58. To Price, Basildon 9/59
34	CFW 212*	Guy Arab II	Roe	L27/28R	From Long 8/58, To Price, Basildon 9/59
35	GV 9866*	Bedford OB	Duple	C29F	From Long 8/58. To Sleeman, London 9/59
36	MMP 815*	Bedford OB	Duple	C29F	From Long 8/58. To Sleeman, London 9/59
40	CCF 120*	AEC Regal III	Duple	C33F	From Long 8/58. To Pearson, Stanmore 9/59
43	DJL 52*	Bedford OB	Duple	C29F	From Long 8/58. To Sleeman, London 9/59

Vehicles acquired but never operated

	NNO 222	Bedford OB	Mulliner	B31F	From Rippingale 5/56. To Baker, Aldershot 5/56
	OEV 889	Bedford OB	Duple	C29F	From Rippingale 5/56. To Tillingbourne Valley, Chilworth; ? Date
	ACF 912	AEC Regal	Thurgood	C35F	From Long 8/58. To Reliance Garage, Norwich; ? Date

LIST 2 - H RIPPINGALE

Livery - Green
Asterisk identifies fleet at sale to Corona

Regn.no.	Chassis type/	Body	Seating	History
PU 500	Ford T	?	? ? ?	New, 9/23. ? disposal
VX 435	Chevrolet	?	B14?	New, 5/29/ ? disposal
VX 1226	Reo Gold	CrownEconomy	B20F	From Hicks, Felstead 11/31 Withdrawn 8/53 (hay store)
UT 3282	?	?	? ? ?	No data
CF 2572	Lancia	?	C16?	From Baldock, Haverhill,? date. Sold 9/35 (showman)
RT 5809	?	?	?14?	From Beeston, East Bertgholt, ?date. Withdrawn 3/39?disposal
EV 237	Chevrolet LO	?	B14F	From Wiffen, Finchingfield, 3/39. Withdrawn 2/51; ? disposal
EV 9057	CommerCentaur	Duple	C20?	From Pyman, Stambourne, 4/46. Withdrawn 8/49 ? disposal
NNO 222*	Bedford OB	Mulliner	B31F	New 6/48. To Corona 5/56 (not operated)
OEV 889*	Bedford OB	Duple	29F	New 3/49. To Corona 5/56 (not operated)
GV 2813	Bedford WLB	Duple	20F	From Osborne, Tollesbury, 8/49. Withdrawn 3/53 (chicken house)
BMR 690*	Bedford WTB		Willmott	C20F From Withers, Chitterne, 3/53. To Corona 5/56
GV 5837*	Bedford WTB		Duple	C26F From Rule, Boxford, 9/53. To Corona 5/56

LIST 3 – A. J. LONG, later E. F. LONG t/a A. J. LONG

Livery - Dark blue and white
Asterisk identifies fleet at sale to Corona

Fleet no.	Regn. number	Chassis type/ builder	Body &c	Seating	History
	CF 8140	? Chevrolet	?	?16?	New 1/28. Burnt out ? date
	CF 8787	?	?	? ? ?	? origin. Withdrawn 1/37. ? disposal
	CF 9968	Crossley	?	C26F	New 6/30. Sold 5/39 (showman)
	TW 8448	?	?	? ? ?	? Origin. ? disposal
	GV 1283	Bedford WLB	Duple	B20?	New 7/32. To Ling, Brockford, ? date
	GV 2364	Dodge	Duple	C20?	New 2/34. ? disposal
12	GV 3029	Gilford 1680T	Wycombe	C32R	New 3/35. Withdrawn 10/49 (caravan)
	VX 1738	?	?	? ? ?	From Bluebird, Tiptree. ? disposal
	BXM 569	Bedford WTL	Duple	C20F	From Mitcham Belle, London.To Honeywood, Stanstead, 4/41
16	GV 5063	AEC Regal	Duple	C35F	New 4/37. Withdrawn 1/55.b ? disposal
	MY 7643	?	?	? ? ?	? origin; ? disposal with date
	UF 5538	Leyland TD1	?	?48?	? origin; ? disposal with date
	GV 7076	Bedford WTB	Duple	C26F	New 6/39; ? disposal with date
	BYG 575	Bedford WTB	?	C25?	From Dickson, Dundee, 9/40. To Central, Sheringham, 8/46
	YG 6600	Leyland LTB5	?	C32R	From Seagull, Great Yarmouth, 3/41. to Simonds, Botesdale, 6/44
	GV 8694	Bedford OWB	?	B32F	New 1/43. Withdrawn 2/52; ? disposal with date 66
	BPE 557	CommerCenturian	?	20?	From Brown, Glemsford, 9/43; To Pye, Blakeney, 4/48
	GV 2536	Dodge	?	B20?	From Brown, Glemsford, 9/43; ? disposal with date
	MV 3433	?	?	?32?	From Brown, Glemsford, 9/43; ? disposal with date
	HX 3569	Gilford	?	?32?	From Brown, Glemsford, 9/43; ? disposal with date
	DR 5803	AEC Regal	?	?36?	From Brown, Glemsford, 9/43; ? disposal with date
	MW 7533	?	?	?20?	From Brown, Glemsford, 9/43; ? disposal with date
	SC 7991	Leyland TS	?	?26?	From Brown, Glemsford, 9/43; To Blackwell, EarlsColne, 8/45
	GO 9647	?	?	?18?	From Brown, Glemsford, 9/43; Withdrawn, 4/45, ? disposal
	WU 9673	?	?	?32?	From Brown, Glemsford, 9/43: Withdrawn, 8/44; ? disposal
	PL 6476	AEC Regal	?	?36?	From Hall, London, 6/44; Withdrawn 2/52, ? disposal
	GV 9454	Bedford OWB	Duple	B30F	New 5/45. To Hipperson, Chelmsford, 11/56 (contractor)
	GV 9866*	Bedford OB	Duple	C29F	New 6/46. To Corona 8/58
	ACF 912*	AEC Regal	Thurgood	C35F	New 2/47. To Corona 8/58
	MMP 815*	Bedford OB	Duple	C29F	From Valliant, London 7/49; To Corona 8/58
	CCF 120*	AEC Regal III	Duple	C33F	New 9/49. To Corona 8/58
	ARU 164	Leyland TD4	Brush	L27/26R	From Hants & Dorset 6/51; Scrapped, 7/58
	DJL 52*	Bedford OB	Duple	C29F	From Flatt, Long Sutton, 1/32; To Corona 8/58
	BEL 395	Leyland TD4c	Brush	L27/26R	From Blackwell, Earls Colne, 3/53; Scrapped 8/55
	CLA 103*	Leyland LT7	ECW	B35R	From Birch Bros., London, 1/55; To Corona 8/58
	BTW 374*	Leyland LT5A	Wilkes & Meade	C35F	From Cansdall, Clacton, 1/55; To Corona 8/58.
	DSG 168*	AEC Regent	Brush	L27/26R	From SMT, 6/55; To Corona 8/58
	GHU 489*	Bristol K5G	Bristol	L26/26R	From Southern Vectis, 1/58; To Corona 9/58
	CFW 212*	Guy Arab II	Roe	L27/28R	From Lincs. Road Car 3/58; to Corona 8/58

Key to seating capacity data	
Subject to data being available, the number of seats is given preceded by:	The number of seats is then followed by:
'B' (bus);	'C' (centre entrance),
'C' (Coach);	'F' (front entrance) or
'L' ('low bridge' double-decker – i.e. with sunken side upper-deck gangway).	'R' (rear entrance).
	Seating for double-deckers indicates first the upper, then the lower saloon.

FLEET PROFILE - CORONA COACHES

Date	Chassis type	Seating Capacity	Number of vehicles	Date	Chassis type	Seating Capacity	Number of vehicles
1 August 1939				**1 May 1957**			
	Bedford WTB	20	1		Bedford OB	29	3
	Leyland KP3	24	1		Bedford HML	29	1
	Leyland KPZ2	25	1		Bedford SB	33	1
	Bedford WTB	25	1		AEC Regal III	33	1
	Leyland KPZ2	26	1		Leyland PS1/1	35	2
	Leyland YS8	32	2		Bedford SBG	38	1
	AEC Regal	32	1		AEC Regal IV	41	1
	Total..	184	8		Total ..	331	10
	Average capacity	23			Average capacity	34	
1 August 1950				**1 September 1958**			
	Bedford WTB	20	1		Bedford OB	29	3
	Leyland KPZ2	25	1		Bedford HML	29	1
	Leyland KPZ2	26	1		AEC Regal III	33	2
	Bedford OB	29	2		Leyland PS1/1	35	2
	Bedford HML	29	1		Leyland LT7	35	1
	Leyland PS1/1	32	1		Leyland LTSA	35	1
	AEC Regal III	33	2		Bedford SBG	38	1
	Leyland PS1/1	35	2		AEC Regal IV	41	1
					AEC Reliance	41	1
	Total ..	326	11		AEC Regent (DD)	55	1
					Guy Arab II (DD)	55	1
	Average capacity	30			Bristol KSG (DD)	56	1
					Total ..	695	19
					Average capacity	37	
1 February 1956					Average capacity, without double-deckers	33	
	Bedford OB	29	3				
	Bedford HML	29	1				
	Bedford SB	33	1				
	AEC Regal III	33	1				
	Leyland PS1/1	35	2				
	Bedford SB	37	1				
	Bedford SBG	38	1				
	AEC Regal IV	41	1				
	Total ..	368	11				
	Average capacity	34					

INTRODUCING SETRIGHT

We took an early decision to replace the 'Belgraphic' ticket machines with 'insert' Setrights, after consulting the road staff. This is a copy of the set of instructions we issued with them.

CORONA COACHES LTD

INSTRUCTIONS TO STAFF for the use of SETRIGHT TICKET MACHINES. 28.5.56.

1. EQUIPMENT: Each Conductor or Driver/Conductor will be issued with a box containing the following equipment. Drivers Plumb and Warner and Conductor Ratcliffe will retain this equipment. All other staff will draw a box, cash-bag and float from the Acton Office before starting duty, and will return same to the Acton Office when paying-in after finishing duty. Staff will sign for equipment and float each time.

Contents of box:
1 Setright Ticket Machine;
1 Breast Plate and Shoulder Strap;
1 Ticket Rack;
Supply of tickets sufficient for the duty;
Supply of Waybills;
Emergency Ticket Book.

2. ISSUE OF TICKETS: The following types of ticket will be in use:-
STAGE SINGLE
STAGE RETURN
EXPRESS SINGLE
EXPRESS DAY-RETURN EXCHANGE
10/- EXPRESS DAY-RETURN

Staff on Services 1, 1A, 1B and 11 will be issued with all types of ticket; Staff on all other Services will be issued with Stage Tickets only.

Issue of Tickets to Passengers:-
A. London Services (1, 1A & 1B). Through passengers to and from Braintree and points to London inclusive will be issued with Express Tickets. Where the Day-Return fare exceeds 11/11d, a 10/- Ticket will be issued, and only the amount in excess of 10/- will be registered on the Ticket. Period Return bookings will be made on the Emergency Ticket Book, the date of return being entered on the ticket. The card copy to be issued to the Passenger and the paper copy to be handed in with the Waybill for Charting. Exchange tickets will be issued against the **return halves** of Office or Agents' Voucher Tickets. Single Voucher Tickets and the outward portion of Returns to be collected and handed in with the Waybill.
B. All other Services. Stage Single and Stage Return Tickets will be all that is required.
C. Luggage, Parcel, Pushchair and Dog Tickets. Gummed 6d Luggage Tickets will be used for the above types of traffic, and issued where necessary in multiples of 6d.
3. USE OF MACHINE: To register a fare, the correct type of ticket must first be inserted in the slot at the font of the machine. Set the wheels as instructed below. Free the handle by releasing the catch below it with one finger, and turn the handle once, allowing the catch to drop back as soon as the handle begins to turn. The handle cannot be turned unless the wheels are set to exact numbers, and the wheels will not turn unless the handle is at rest.

Before starting the duty set the month and date wheels correctly.
On entering each stage set the stage wheels.
Before registering each fare set the cash wheels.
SPECIAL CARE must be taken in setting the cash wheels, to avoid registering more cash than has been received from the passenger.
To cancel a Setright Return, or issue an Exchange proceed as above, but set the cash wheels to zero. The machine then records one no-value on the left-hand top counter for each turn of the wheel. Returns should be cancelled at the opposite end, as indicated on the ticket.
4. COMPLETION OF THE WAYBILL: Before starting the duty, enter on the front of the Waybill the opening numbers of the Machine Counters (No-Value), Total Tickets, Shillings, and Pence); the opening numbers of each type of Ticket (including Luggage Tickets), and the opening number of the Emergency Ticket Book. This information will be entered against the word 'Start', and at the end of the duty, the closing numbers will be entered against the word 'Finish'. A simple substraction sum then gives the total for each entry, and the number of Tickets issued and amount of cash due can be easily obtained. Ten Shillings multiplied by the number of 10/- Day-Return Tickets sold must be included in the Cash Total, together with Sixpence multiplied by the number of Luggage Tickets sold.
The same entries must be made on the back of the Waybill for each journey. Each column should be entered up **before the end of the journey**, and the opening numbers of the next journey entered at the same time. The total cash due as shown on the front and on the back of the Waybill must agree.
5. SPOILT TICKETS: If a ticket is wrongly issued, it should be retained and attached to the Waybill when paying in. In cases of genuine error, the amount shown on such a ticket will be treated as cash, and deducted from the amount due on the Waybill. The most usual errors, which Staff are requested to avoid, are: (1) Registering single fare on return ticket or vice versa; (2) Failing to return Shillings wheel to zero before issuing a fare of less than 1/-. With care and practice, these errors can be avoided.
Should it prove impossible to insert a return ticket for cancellation the ticket should be mutilated so as to be unusable, and the machine operated at 'no-value'.

SERVICE NUMBERS (With effect from 14th May 1956)	
1	Stowmarket - Sudbury - Halstead - London (Express)
1A	Hadleigh - Sudbury - Halstead - London (Express)
1B	Hartest - Sudbury - Halstead - London (Express)
6	Sudbury - Acton - Monks Eleigh - Ipswich
7	Wattisham RAF Station - London (Express)
11	Stowmarket - Bildeston - Lavenham - Sudbury - Halstead
17	Gestingthorpe - Yeldham - Toppesfield - Braintree
18	Gestingthorpe - Belchamp Walter - Sudbury
19	Gestingthorpe - Wickham St. Paul - Sudbury
19A	Sudbury Bulmer - Sudbury Circular
20	Belchamp Walter - Wickham St. Paul - Halstead
21	Sudbury - Twinstead - Pebmarch - Halstead
22	Lavenham - Acton - Waldingfield - Sudbury
23	Sudbury - Acton - Sudbury Circular
97	Maplestead - Halstead School Service
98	Foxearth - Halstead - Earls Colne School Service
99	Sudbury - Gestingthorpe - Yeldham Works Service

SERVICE NUMBERS AND ROUTE CHANGES

Note: In the left hand column is the company's service number. This is followed (in brackets) by the Traffic Commissioners' licence number (which would be preceded by F/R 16/). The company's policy was to use numbers below 11 for express carriage services and to number contract services from 99 down

Service No	(Licence No)	Terminals and route details, with alterations
1	(7)	STOWMARKET Barnard's Garage and LONDON Kings Cross Coach Station *via Bildeston, Lavenham, Sudbury, Halstead & Chelmsford. Daily. [Stowmarket terminal renamed Station Road, with no change, 23.3.59]*
1A	(9)	HADLEIGH Market Place and LONDON Kings Cross Coach Station *via Sudbury, Halstead & Chelmsford. Daily.*
1B	(8)	HARTEST The Green and LONDON Kings Cross Coach Station *via Sudbury, Halstead & Chelmsford. Daily. [Extended to commence at REDE Council Houses, 29.1.58. Renumbered 4, commencing at BURY ST EDMUNDS Angel Hill, 18.8.58] Daily.*
2	(31)	*Number provisionally allocated to Blackwell's service (see pp xx-xx)*
4	(8)	BURY ST EDMUNDS Angel Hill & LONDON Kings Cross Coach Station *[using journeys on Service 12 (16/35) between Bury St . Edmunds & Rede - commenced 18.8.58, previously Service 1B] Daily.*
6	(11)	SUDBURY Old Market Place and IPSWICH Half Moon & Star, *St. Matthew's Street via Long Melford, Little Waldingfield & Monks Eleigh. [Renumbered 16 as stage carriage, with diversion, 3/7/56, see below] Daily.*
7	(20)	WATTISHAM RAF Station & LONDON Kings Cross Coach Station *[joint with W J Cooper (later Combs Coaches Ltd) & B A Taylor & Sons]* Weekends as required for leave.
11	(17)	STOWMARKET Barnard's Garage & HALSTEAD The Bull *via Bildeston, Lavenham & Sudbury. (All service 1 express timings also appeared on the timetable) [Sudbury-Halstead section transferred to Service 21, 17.6.57] Daily (terminating at Sudbury on Sundays).*
11	(12)	STOWMARKET Barnard's Garage & SUDBURY Old Market Place *via Bildeston & Lavenham. [Curtailed service introduced 17.6.57 with diversion via Preston St Mary (not Sundays); journeys not by standard route transferred to Service 22, but reverted to Service 11 23.3.59; Stowmarket terminal renamed Station Road, with no change, 23.3.59; diversion via Combs Ford (not Sundays)] (Service 1 timings remained on timetable). Daily.*
12	(35)	CLARE Market Hill & BURY ST EDMUNDS Angel Hill *via Stansfield & Rede. (ex Long 18.8.58). [Certain journeys connected with Service 4 (see above); certain journeys linked with Services 13 & 14, ?.?.59, to provide through services Clare-Sudbury via Thurston End, Thursdays & Fridays] Daily.*
13	(36)	CAVENDISH The George & BURY ST EDMUNDS Angel Hill *(ex & 33) Long 18.8.58) via Glemsford, Boxted, Rede & Horringer Wednesdays or via Glemsford, Stansfield & Rede Wednesdays & Saturdays) [Certain journeys linked with services 12 & 14 to provide through Clare-Sudbury Service via Thurston End, see above]. Licence 16/36 surrendered 14.9.59.*
14	(32)	GLEMSFORD Broadway & SUDBURY Old Market Place or Cornard Road *via Glemsford (Three Turns) & Long Melford. (ex Long 18.8.58) Daily.*
15	(32)	CLARE Market Hill & SUDBURY Old Market Place, *Market Hill or Cornard Road via Cavendish, Glemsford (Three Turns), Glemsford (Broadway), Stanstead (White Hart) & Long Melford. (ex Long 18.8.58) Daily. [Journey extended to Sudbury (Railway Station), ? ?.58; certain journeys linked with services 12 & 13 to provide hrough Clare-Sudbury service via Thurston End, see above). Daily.*
16	(11)	SUDBURY Old Market Place & IPSWICH Half Moon & Star , *St Matthew's Street via Long Melford, Little Waldingfield, Monks Eleigh & Lindsey Tye. [Commenced 3/7/56, previously Service 6, see above Commenced at Glemsford 27.1.59, see below] Tuesdays.*
16	(11)	GLEMSFORD Broadway & IPSWICH Grey Green Depot. *Old Foundry Road via Glemsford (Three Turns), Long Melford, Sudbury, Acton, Little Waldingfield, Monks Eleigh & Lindsey Tye. [Commenced 27.1.59, see above] Tuesdays.*
17	(26)	GESTINGTHORPE & BRAINTREE Bus Park *via Little Yeldham, Great Yeldham, Toppesfield & Gainsford End (ex Rippingale 15.5.56) [Revised & extended 12.11.56, see below] Wednesdays*
17	(26)	SUDBURY Old Market Place & BRAINTREE Bus Park *via Borley Green, Belchamp Walter, Gestingthorpe, Little Yeldham, Great Yeldham, Toppesfield & Gainsford End, Wednesdays or via Bulmer, Gestingthorpe, Little Yeldham, Great Yeldham & Gainsford End, Saturdays. [From 12.11.56, see above. Saturday service suspended, 2.2.57-?.?.57. Gainsford End spur abandoned 4.12.57 & Saturday service withdrawn, see below]*
17	(26)	SUDBURY Old Market Place & BRAINTREE Bus Park *via Bulmer, Gestingthorpe, Belchamp Walter, Little Yeldham, Great Yeldham & Toppesfield. [From 4.12.57, see above. Return tickets between Great Yeldham & Braintree inter-available with B K Jennings] Wednesdays*
18	(24)	GESTINGTHORPE Foundry Corner & SUDBURY Market Hill *via Little Yeldham (Thursdays only), Belchamp Walter & Borley (omitted on some journeys). (ex Rippingale 15.5.56) [Revised & merged with 16/23, 14.11.56] Wednesdays, Thursdays & Saturdays.*
18	(23)	GESTINGTHORPE Foundry Corner & SUDBURY Old Market Place *via Little Yeldham, Belchamp Walter & Ballingdon [Detached from 16/24, 14.11.56; but this number was used to cover anti-clockwise journeys on 16/23 1.5.59] Tuesdays, Thursdays & Saturdays.*
19	(23)	GESTINGTHORPE & SUDBURY Market Hill *via Wickham St Pauls (omitted on some journeys), Long Gardens (omitted on some journeys) & Bulmer. (ex Rippingale 15.5.56) [Revised & merged with 16/24 13.11.56] Tuesdays, Thursdays & Saturdays.*
19	(23)	SUDBURY Old Market Place & SUDBURY Old Market Place, *circular via Bulmer, (some journeys via Finch Hill, Thursdays & Saturdays), Wickham St Paul (omitted on some journeys), Gestingthorpe, Belchamp Walter & Borley (omitted on some journeys). Tuesdays, Thursdays & Saturdays 13.5.56; Wednesdays, Thursdays & Saturdays 19.6.57. [Spur to Henny, Clay Hills, Thursdays introduced 19.6.57. Became 18 (anti-clockwise) & 19 (clockwise), Thursdays, Saturdays & Sundays, ?.?.59, with Henny Spur transferred to Service 21]*
19A	(27)	SUDBURY Market Hill & SUDBURY Market Hill *via Bulmer Tye, The Cedars, Smeetham Hall Lane & Finch Hill (anti-clockwise only). (ex Rippingale 15.5.56). [Merged with 16/23 15.11.56] Thursdays.*
20	(25)	BELCHAMP WALTER & HALSTEAD The Bull *via Gestingthorpe & Wickham St Pauls [from Gestingthorpe only on Fridays] (ex Rippingale 15.5.56) Extended to commence at Sudbury, Old Market Place, 13.11.56] Tuesdays & Fridays.*
20	(25)	SUDBURY Old Market Place & HALSTEAD Bull *via Ballingdon, Belchamp Walter, Gestingthorpe & Wickham St Pauls [from 13.11.56, see above] Tuesdays & Fridays.*
21	(21)	SUDBURY Market Hill & HALSTEAD Bull *via Bulmer & Maplestead, Saturdays [Certain journeys diverted via Pebmarsh & Sudbury terminal moved to Old Market Place, 2.6.56. Certain journeys diverted via Wickham St Paul & frequency extended to Mondays to Saturdays, 12.11.56. Service 1 timings added to licence (see above), 17.6.57. Henny Spur, Thursdays, transferred from Service 19 (16/23), 8.6.59]*

| 22 | 17 | LAVENHAM Swan & SUDBURY Market Hill *via Harwood Place & Acton,* Wednesdays & Saturdays. *[Additional journeys including Great Waldingfield added; Sudbury terminal moved to Old Market Place with frequency extended to* Mondays to Saturdays, *23.4.56; Extended to commence at Bildeston, 17.6.57]* |

| 22 | 17 | BILDESTON Market Place & SUDBURY Old Market Place *(see above) via Monks Eleigh, Lavenham, Acton & Great Waldingfield. [Journeys beyond Monks Eleigh limited to Wednesday evening picture bus. All journeys reverted to Service 11 (16/17), 21.4.59]* Mondays to Saturdays. |

| 23 | (4) | ACTON Crown & SUDBURY Market Hill *via Great Waldingfield [Certain journeys commenced at Newmans Green & relief worked Sudbury-Newmans Green-Acton. Revised as circular 23.4.56, see below]* Thursdays & Saturdays *(but Saturday journeys were not operated).* |

| 23 | (4) | SUDBURY Old Market Place & SUDBURY Old Market Place *circular via Newmans Green, Acton & Great Waldingfield [from 23.4.56, see above]* Mondays to Saturdays. |

| 29 | (30) | GREAT MAPLESTEAD School & SUDBURY Old Market Place *via Gestingthorpe & either Belchamp Walter & Borley or Bulmer. [Extension of existing journeys on Service 19 (16/23), 3.5.58]* Saturdays. |

| 30 | (32) | CLARE Market Hill & CLARE Market Hill *circular, via Cavendish, Glemsford (Three Turns), Glemsford (Broadway), Long Melford, Sudbury, Gestingthorpe, Castle Hedingham, Sible Hedingham (Rippers' Works), Great Yeldham, Tilbury & Ovington [complete circle covered only clockwise] (ex Long 18.8.58) [One journey diverted via Wickham St Paul, Saturdays, ?.?.59]* Mondays to Saturdays. |

| 97 | (—) | MAPLESTEAD & HALSTEAD - *Essex School Contract, one vehicle (ex Rippingale 15.5.56) Not renewed, ?.9.56.* |

| 98 | (—) | FOXEARTH & EARLS COLNE - *Essex School Contract, one vehicle (ex Rippingale 15.5.56) Not renewed, ?.9.56.* |

| 98 | (28) | ACTON The Crown & GREAT YELDHAM (Whitlocks' Works) *via Clare. Restricted to employees of Messrs Whitlock. From 15.10.56.* |

| 99 | (29) | SUDBURY Market Hill & GREAT YELDHAM (Whitlocks' Works) *via Gestingthorpe & Castle Hedingham. Restricted to employees of Messrs Whitlock. (ex Rippingale 15.5.56, licensed 15.10.56)* |

| — | (—) | GLEMSFORD & CLARE via Cavendish - *West Suffolk School Contract, one double-decker & one saloon (ex Long 18.8.58)* |

| — | (—) | CLARE & SUDBURY via Cavendish, *Glemsford & Stanstead - West Suffolk School Contract, one saloon from Clare & Cavendish & one saloon from Glemsford & Stanstead (ex Long 18.8.58)* |

| — | (—) | HEDINGHAM & STOKE-BY-CLARE Grenville College *via Yeldham & Ashen - private contract with Grenville College (ex Long 18.8.58)* |

| — | (—) | HEDINGHAM & GLEMSFORD via Sudbury - *private contract with Messrs Rippers, operated when overtime worked at the factory (ex Long 18.8.58)* |

| — | (6) | EXCURSIONS & TOURS *originating at SUDBURY Old Market Place. Picking-up points also at Long Melford, Acton, Little Waldingfield, Great Waldingfield & Lavenham. Additional points added at [1] Brent Eleigh & Monks Eleigh (certain destinations only); [2] Bulmer Tye, Twinstead Cross Roads, Catley Cross & Little Maplestead (on tours routed via A.131); Glemsford (Three Turns), Cavendish & Clare (on tours routed via A.1092). Maximum of three vehicles on any one day, with one additionally for afternoon & evening tours.* |

| — | (22) | EXCURSIONS & TOURS *originating at GESTINGTHORPE Foundry Corner with additional picking up points at Bulmer Tye, Bulmer Village, Wickham St Paul, Belchamp Walter, Twinstead Village & Little Maplestead Village. Maximum of two vehicles on any one day. (ex Rippingale 15.5.56)* |

| — | (34) | EXCURSIONS & TOURS *originating at LONG MELFORD Burtons Farm with sundry picking up points in Long Melford. Maximum of three vehicles in any one day. (ex Long 18.8.58)* |

| — | (37) | EXCURSIONS & TOURS *originating at GLEMSFORD The Broadway with sundry picking up points in Glemsford. Maximum of two vehicles on any one day. (ex Long 18.8.58)* |

| — | (38) | EXCURSIONS & TOURS *originating at FENSTEAD END Hooks Hall with additional picking up points at Thurston End, Stansfield, Poslingford, Clare & Cavendish. Maximum of four vehicles on any one day. (ex Long 18.8.58)* |

TICKETS

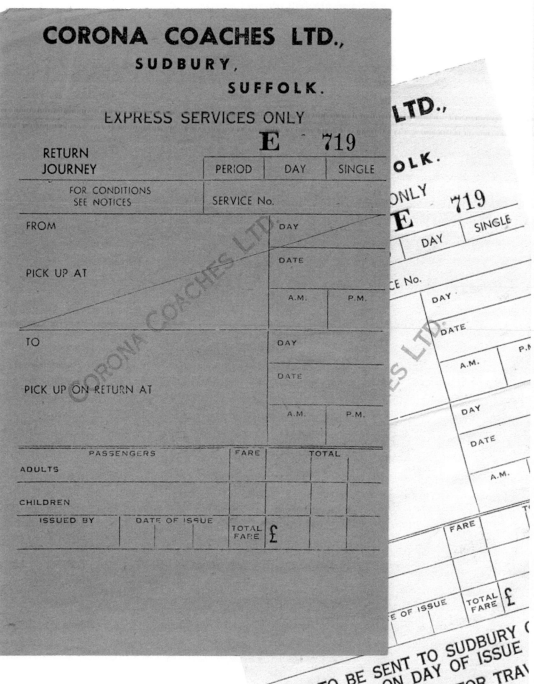

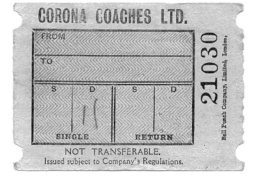

ABOVE: Express service voucher tickets.

LEFT: 'Belgraphic' ticket, issued through machine.

RIGHT: Plain 'Willebrew' tickets as carried in case of failure of a Belgraphic machine.

ABOVE: The full range of 'Setright' insert tickets
BELOW: Some advertising carried on the reverse of Setright tickets.

No: 2815

CORONA
COACHES
PARCEL
PAID

1/-

No. 1716

CORONA
COACHES
PARCEL
PAID

4d.

No: 1614

8d

Corona
Coaches Ltd.
Parcels
Service

COMPANY NOT RESPONSIBLE
IF PARCELS ARE LOST
DAMAGED OR DELAYED.

Bell Punch Company, Limited, London. 6-53

No. 1614

CORONA
COACHES LTD.
PREPAID PARCELS
RECEIPT

8d

COMPANY NOT RESPONSIBLE
IF PARCELS ARE LOST.
DAMAGED OR DELAYED.
Bell Punch Company, Limited, London.

2612

3d

Corona
Coaches Ltd.
Parcels
Service

COMPANY NOT RESPONSIBLE
IF PARCELS ARE LOST
DAMAGED OR DELAYED.

Bell Punch Company, Limited, London.

0220

Corona
Coaches Ltd.
Parcels
Service

1/-

COMPANY NOT RESPONSIBLE
IF PARCELS ARE LOST
DAMAGED OR DELAYED.

Bell Punch Company, Limited, London. 6-53

4d

0512

ABOVE: Reecipts for parcels carried on Corona bus services.
BELOW: Tickets for S. Brown's services, sold to Long in 1943.

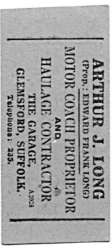

ABOVE and LEFT: Tickets for Long's services (E. F. Long, trading as A. J. Long).

ANOTHER COUNTRY BUSMAN

WILLIAM GEORGE AMOS
(J. AMOS & SON) of Belchamp St Paul

The chopping services to Sudbury ran for the last time on Tuesday, 31st December 2002 with the retirement at the age of 80 of W. G. (Billy) Amos. Other activities had ceased earlier in the year. Latterly the service had operated once each way as follows:

Knowl Green – Sudbury Bus Station via Belchamp St Paul, Pentlow and Foxearth – Tuesdays.

Ovington, Green – Sudbury Bus Station via Belchamp St Paul, Belchamp Otten, Borley Green and Borley – Thursdays.

Ovington, Green – Sudbury Bus Station via Tilbury Juxta Clare, Great Yeldham, Little Yeldham, Knowl Green, Belchamp St Paul, Pentlow and Foxearth – Saturdays.

This was the last surviving small family business in the area which started as a carrier. James Amos, Billy's father had been in business as a shopkeeper and carrier from his home village of Belchamp St Paul on the Essex/Suffolk border to Sudbury, seven miles to the south east, on Tuesdays and Thursdays by 1906. Daniel Amos had worked this route at the end of the previous century. Early activities included the conveyance of passengers to the local railway stations at Clare, Cavendish, Great Yeldham and Sudbury. The motor replaced the horses in the early 1920s and the business developed to include haulage and cattle carrying.

In 1931 a licence was acquired from the Traffic Commissioners to continue the Thursday shopping service from Ovington to Sudbury via Belchamp St Paul and Belchamp Otten and a Saturday evening service between the same points via Belchamp St Paul and Pentlow. A licence was also obtained for an excursion from Belchamp St Paul to Clacton-on-Sea. For a short while in 1936 a Tuesday evening pictures bus was operated between Ovington and Cavendish via Tilbury Juxta Clare, Knowl Green, Belchamp St Paul and Pentlow and during the summer of 1938 a Saturday service was operated between Belchamp St Paul and Halstead via Ovington, Tilbury Juxta Clare, Little Yeldham, North End and Gestingthorpe. In 1939 authority was received for the Saturday evening service to Sudbury to pick up additionally at Foxearth.

In 1947 a Saturday afternoon service between Ovington and Sudbury via Belchamp St Paul, Pentlow and Foxearth and Wednesday and Sunday evening services between Belchamp St Paul and Sudbury via Pentlow and Foxearth were introduced. From 1948 these new services operated via Tilbury Juxta Clare and Knowl Green and from 1951 also Great and Little Yeldham. The Wednesday, Saturday and Sunday evening services were withdrawn in 1965, by which time most households had television and evening trips into town for the pictures and other entertainment were less popular. Also in 1948 the Thursday afternoon service to Sudbury was diverted via Borley and a Wednesday service was introduced between Ovington and Bury St Edmunds via Tilbury Juxta Clare, Great Yeldham, Little Yeldham, Knowl Green, Belchamp St Paul, Pentlow and Foxearth which continued until 1968. Early in 1950 a Tuesday service was introduced between Ovington and Halstead via Tilbury Juxta Clare, Knowl Green, Belchamp St Paul, Pentlow, Foxearth, Borley, Bulmer and Bulmer Tye. This service was diverted via Sudbury from 1957 and curtailed at Sudbury in 1965. During 1966 a Weekday peak service was introduced between Ovington and Sudbury via Tilbury Juxta Clare, Great Yeldham, Little Yeldham, Knowl Green, Belchamp St Paul, Pentlow and Foxearth, but this was short-lived. The services were transferred into the joint names of James and W. G. Amos in 1954 and into the sole name of W. G. Amos in 1965. By August 2000 the Tuesday service only was only operating between Knowl Green and Sudbury no longer serving Ovington, Tilbury Juxta Clare or Borley.

As was the case with most small operators in the 1920s, a 14-seat Ford Model 'T' was owned followed by two 14-seat Chevrolets, but in 1938 a 20-seat Duple bodied Bedford WLB was acquired from Thorp Bros of West Mersea and thereafter many of the vehicles owned were coaches of Bedford manufacture. The last journey with Billy Amos at the wheel as usual and three Omnibus Society members on board was performed by an ex-Brighton Transport Dodge with 25-seat Alexander body (D457 YPN) acquired in 1998.

Not withstanding his 'retirement', W. G. (Billy) Amos subsequently passed his medical and in January 2003 was driving a school bus for a neighbouring operator!

Peter Clark, 9 March 2003
With acknowledgement to The Omnibus Society